SOUL FORCE

"*If you want to unleash the power of change in your life and community, this book is a road map.*"
—LEROY BARBER, EXECUTIVE DIRECTOR OF THE VOICES PROJECT

"*A useful, compelling guide to an alternative life. . . . Readers will be strengthened and encouraged.*"
—WALTER BRUEGGEMANN, THEOLOGIAN AND AUTHOR OF *THE PROPHETIC IMAGINATION*

"*A powerful reminder, guide, and source of sustenance for all those who seek abundant life for themselves and for their community.*"
—ALEXIA SALVATIERRA, PASTOR AND COAUTHOR OF *FAITH-ROOTED ORGANIZING*

"Soul Force *calls us to pivot and to turn the tide of ecclesial dysfunction. . . . Offers the possibility that cynicism can pivot toward hope.*"
—SOONG-CHAN RAH, PROFESSOR OF CHURCH GROWTH AND EVANGELISM AT NORTH PARK THEOLOGICAL SEMINARY

"*This book is about* soul force, *which has the power to change the world, overthrow tyranny, break every chain, and set both the oppressed and oppressors free.*"
—SHANE CLAIBORNE, ACTIVIST AND AUTHOR OF *THE IRRESISTIBLE REVOLUTION*

"Soul Force *is a clear call to action . . . reminding us that small, intentional pivots can make significant change.*"
—MICHELLE WARREN, AUTHOR OF *THE POWER OF PROXIMITY*

"A great tool for emerging and seasoned community leaders, moving from negatives to energizing reframes that build healthy communities."
—MARY NELSON, ACTIVIST AND COMMUNITY ORGANIZER

"Astonishing in its sophistication and practicality. . . . This is a revolutionary guidebook to community development."
—MARK SCANDRETTE, COAUTHOR OF *FREE*

"In an age plagued by hopelessness . . . we desperately need 'fire starters': people who relight our souls. This book is the spark we have been looking for."
—JOHN MCKNIGHT, COAUTHOR OF *THE ABUNDANT COMMUNITY*

"Soul Force points us all toward the individual, communal, and systemic pivots necessary for revealing the world of which we have always dreamed."
—JONATHAN BROOKS, AUTHOR OF *CHURCH FORSAKEN*

"A prophetic work that invites us all into a movement that reshapes how we understand community and connection."
—ROZELLA HAYDÉE WHITE, SPEAKER, WRITER, AND LIFE COACH

"Soul Force is what we need—and we need it right now!"
—PAUL SPARKS, COAUTHOR OF *THE NEW PARISH*

"A must-read for all who are serious about personal and community transformation."
—AVA STEAFFENS, CEO OF CHRISTIAN COMMUNITY DEVELOPMENT ASSOCIATION

"This book is the good news that the watching world is desperate for."
—JER SWIGART, COFOUNDING DIRECTOR OF THE GLOBAL IMMERSION PROJECT

SOUL FORCE

*Seven Pivots toward
Courage, Community, and Change*

REESHEDA
GRAHAM-WASHINGTON

SHAWN
CASSELBERRY

HERALD
P R E S S

Harrisonburg, Virginia

Herald Press
PO Box 866, Harrisonburg, Virginia 22803
www.HeraldPress.com

Library of Congress Cataloging-in-Publication Data
Names: Graham-Washington, Reesheda, author.
Title: Soul force : seven pivots toward courage, community, and change /
  Reesheda Graham-Washington, Shawn Casselberry.
Description: Harrisonburg : Herald Press, 2018.
Identifiers: LCCN 2018002095| ISBN 9781513803036 (pbk. : alk. paper) |
  ISBN
  9781513803043 (hardcover : alk. paper)
Subjects: LCSH: Social justice--Religious aspects. | Conduct of life.
Classification: LCC BL65.J87 G73 2018 | DDC 248.4--dc23 LC record avail-
able at https://lccn.loc.gov/2018002095

SOUL FORCE
© 2018 by Herald Press, Harrisonburg, Virginia 22803. 800-245-7894.
  All rights reserved.
Library of Congress Control Number: 2018002095
International Standard Book Number: 978-1-5138-0303-6 (paperback);
978-1-5138-0305-0 (ebook); 978-1-5138-0304-3 (hardcover)
Printed in United States of America
Cover and interior design by Reuben Graham

Unless otherwise noted, Scripture text is quoted, with permission, from the
New Revised Standard Version, © 1989, Division of Christian Education of
the National Council of Churches of Christ in the United States of America,
and the *American Standard Version*, public domain.

22 21 20 19 18   10 9 8 7 6 5 4 3 2 1

In this fiftieth-year commemoration of the assassination of the Reverend Dr. Martin Luther King Jr., we dedicate this book to the legacy of Dr. King, Mahatma Gandhi, and the unseen movement makers who keep their spirits alive.

CONTENTS

soul force (noun):

1. a spiritual energy, a vital force conceived of as constituting, residing in, or emanating from the soul[1]
2. from the Hindi word *satyagraha*, composed of two Sanskrit words: *satya*, meaning "truth and love," and *agraha*, meaning "firmness" or "force"
3. a method of nonviolent resistance inspired by the life of Jesus and developed and practiced by Mahatma Gandhi and Dr. Martin Luther King

---

1. First definition from *The Oxford English Dictionary*. The second definition was compiled from various sources; the third is a definition by the authors.

AN ENTRY INTO
SOUL FORCE

Again and again we must rise to the majestic heights of meeting physical force with soul force.
—MARTIN LUTHER KING JR., "I HAVE A DREAM," AUGUST 28, 1963

The sunlight on Robben Island is exceedingly bright as it reflects off limestone. A thirty-minute ferry ride from Cape Town, South Africa, on the mainland, Robben Island is the site of the high-security prison where Nelson Mandela spent eighteen years for his opposition to the apartheid system. The quarry where prisoners like Mandela once labored still exists. There, in an unrelenting sun so bright that it actually blinded some prisoners, Mandela and other political prisoners and dissidents dug up and broke apart rocks in hard labor that is difficult for us to imagine.

We had both traveled to South Africa with a group of national faith leaders to dialogue with South African leaders about the common struggles we faced. We were both feeling tired, emotionally and physically, from the community work we were each doing in Chicago, where we both run national nonprofits. Yet here we were, having traveled nineteen hours to the tip of the African continent to find some inspiration. We visited several faith communities and met brilliant women and men who were doing innovative work. Although apartheid had formally ended twenty years earlier, the effects of poverty and racial segregation were still very much apparent. The apartheid system had economically depleted Black and colored communities, in many cases robbing them of their land and livelihoods and creating a vacuum that was currently being filled by drug trafficking, prostitution, and gang activity. While learning this history and hearing people's stories, we saw many parallels with the issues plaguing our own city.

We were feeling the weight of all this when we arrived at Robben Island, not fully prepared for what we were about to encounter. Walking the island, we tried to imagine what it must have been like to be restrained on this small strip of land for so long. We visited the cell where Mandela spent most of his time; it was about the size of a small bathroom. And we heard stories of abuse by guards and how the apartheid system was maintained even within the prison, with Black prisoners receiving fewer food rations than "coloreds," or those who were of mixed racial heritage.[2]

Given this backdrop, we were astounded that Mandela not only survived Robben Island but left with no chip of bitterness on his shoulder. He offered forgiveness for the brutal oppression he endured as a result of the ignorance and greed of the white ruling class. Not only that—he led the country into a place of national forgiveness and unity. While Mandela was far from perfect and South Africa still has many challenges, his witness remains a tangible example of the power of reconciliation for our divided world.

On Robben Island we found our inspiration. This experience led us to a deeper examination of our own hearts and an exploration of the faith and lives of courageous people throughout history. We began asking questions like:

Where does courage come from?

What caused a lowly shepherd boy with a slingshot to go up against a towering giant?

---

2. We have opted to capitalize the word *Black* when referring to race or ethnicity throughout the book. For the case for Black with a capital *B*, see Lori L. Tharps, "The Case for Black with a Capital B," *The New York Times*, November 18, 2014, https://www.nytimes.com/2014/11/19/opinion/the-case-for-black-with-a-capital-b.html.

What caused a young leader to keep marching around a city until the walls came down?

What caused a privileged queen to risk her position, and possibly her life, to advocate for her people?

What caused a humble girl of little means and influence to say yes to bearing a child who was destined to save the world?

What caused a brash disciple to step out of a boat in a raging storm while the other disciples stayed in the boat?

What caused the widow in Jesus' parable to persist until she won justice from an unjust judge?

What caused Jesus to face the violence of the cross and offer forgiveness for the very ones who crucified him?

Or African slaves to sing and keep hope in the midst of hundreds of years of brutal slavery and oppression?

What caused a little girl to write in a diary in the middle of a holocaust?

Or an unassuming Indian religious teacher to challenge the British Empire through nonviolent resistance?

Or a Black Baptist preacher from the Deep South to show love in the face of racial hatred and bigotry?

The easy answer is "God." But that would require assuming that everyone else around them *didn't* have God. It would mean these people's actions didn't require something on their part—a posture and a persistence that enabled them to find strength and resolve when others cowered. Each of them tapped into something extra inside. They found a courage—an internal conviction and resolve—to act in faith and hope despite their fears.

It's easy to think that this kind of courage and power is restricted to biblical times or the virtue of the most saintly or heroic among us. But all over the world, people have risen up to resist, create, forgive, advocate, and bear witness to love in the most distressing and depressing of life's circumstances. Somehow they have not let fear, insecurity, or opposition keep them from pressing onward. In the face of hurt and violence and despair, they find power within to resist cynicism, love their neighbors, and not return evil for evil.

They channeled their soul force. Discovering and developing the practice of soul force can make it possible for us to do the same.

WHAT IS SOUL FORCE?

The concept of soul force derives from the Hindi word *satyagraha*. Composed of two Sanskrit words—*satya*, which means "truth" or "love," both of which are often attributed to the soul, and *agraha*, which means "polite insistence," "holding firmly to," or "force"—*satyagraha* is a philosophy of nonviolent resistance that was rooted in the teachings of Jesus.[3] Mohandas Gandhi (often called Mahatma, an honorific meaning "great soul") developed the idea in the Indian context, and Martin Luther King Jr. further refined and claimed it for the civil rights movement in the United States.

Historically, we have seen giants in civil rights apply the power of soul force to social movements, political activism, and socioeconomics. But it can also be applied to our daily lives in whatever location, vocation, or season we are experiencing. Exerting soul force requires us to name and know our true identities, live out our truth courageously and unapologetically, and hold firmly to all of who we are. When we start to meander away from our true identities, soul force requires us to insist on the truth.

Soul force is where the Spirit of God and our human resilience meet. The Spirit doesn't override our will, nor does it bypass our humanity. The Spirit works in concert and collaboration with our ingenuity, gifts, and grit. Soul force is a power that emerges when we align with the Spirit of truth, love, and liberation. Soul force is an awakening to the realization that we have a creative force within us, because we all bear the divine imprint of the Creator. But so rarely do we tap into this power.

---

3. Louis Fischer, *Gandhi: His Life and Message for the World* (New York: Signet, 1953), 35–40. Our understanding of soul force is heavily influenced by Martin Luther King's six principles of nonviolence and Mahatma Gandhi's philosophy of *satyagraha*. In his 1958 book *Stride toward Freedom: The Montgomery Story*, King outlined six fundamental tenets of nonviolence. These principles are related to soul force in that they illustrate the posture necessary to tap into individual and collective soul force. When we act out of anger, pain, or resentment, we often choose to identify violent solutions. When we reach beyond our initial frustration and go deeper, accessing our soul force, we discover a more enduring, redemptive way of being together.

Soul force is an inner alignment with truth, a fortified internal strength that creates the capacity for courage and change in the face of great adversity. Soul force is a courageous, compassionate love that leads to personal and social transformation. Gandhi and King utilized soul force in their contexts to ignite movements for social change, and we can utilize it for movement in our lives too.

So what does soul force look like for the rest of us? What does soul force look like for the teacher who shows up every day for her students? The nonprofit leader trying to do good in the community on a shoestring budget? The neighborhood matriarch who faithfully tends the community garden? The pastor who feels burnt out from carrying the needs of his congregation? The parents who stay up late worrying about their kids?

Soul force is just as needed for everyday struggles of life as it is for larger social change. Soul force is not reserved for the few saints among us. It is an energy that each of us has the capacity to tap into and develop.

Soul force is needed now more than ever.

YOU ALREADY HAVE IT

It is important to underscore soul force's "already existence," which is to say that we do not have to do anything to create it. It is also important to note its internal way of being. Soul force comes from within, from inside us. Jesus told his disciples, "The kingdom of God is within you" (Luke 17:21 ASV). They didn't need to look outside themselves to find God or to access God's power. In the same way, soul force is already and always accessible to us.

The idea of soul force as internal is critical to the way we understand it, as its internal nature is so contrary to who we have become as a society. We live in a context that tells us to only believe what we can see: that which is tangible. So much of who we are and what we do is external, and so much of what we use to define, energize, and mobilize ourselves comes from outside ourselves. We attempt to discover who we are through our acquisition of titles, promotions, achievements, and recognition from outside ourselves. We attempt to achieve comfort and safety through the acquisition of material things such as money, houses, and cars. We attempt to find rest by binging on social and mass media that are focused on others and that often rile us up rather than create true moments of rest. There is nothing wrong with any of these elements in their own right. Yet when we use them as distractions or replacements for true identity, peace, and rest—which can only come from a connection with soul force—we cheat ourselves out of the opportunity to be true to who we are and who we have the capacity to become.

The idiosyncratic nature of soul force is such that we must trust in its existence *before* we can maximize its existence. Because soul force is a spiritual energy, it does not take on a form until we manifest it through our courage to live the truth. In order for soul force to influence our lives, we must trust that it lives within us, and we must live as though it lives within us. Only then will we witness its impact.

SOUL FORCE ON THE MOUNT

The good news is that we don't have to create soul force. It is already there, ready to be accessed by each one of us. And the even greater news is that we get to harness it, galvanize it, and direct it toward our own individual and communal brilliance.

Before the disciples could light up the world with the truth and love of Christ, they had to believe they were the light of the world. Their responsibility was not to manufacture light, but to live in line with the light that lived inside them. They had to believe they were capable of shining their light for the world to see. In the Sermon on the Mount, Jesus told them what it looked like to be a light in an evil and unjust world (Matthew 5:3-48). It meant being a witness to another kingdom, one that prioritized the poor, that hungered for justice, that worked diligently for peace, that did the right thing even when it was costly. Jesus was introducing them to a way of being and living that reflected God's *agape* love and peace.

The religious people of Jesus' day had become content with religiosity. They had become conditioned to the patterns and value systems of their culture. They needed a radical reorientation and realignment to love, compassion, nonviolence, and righteous justice seeking. They needed to understand that love overcomes fear, breaks cycles of violence, relieves economic anxieties, and liberates from status quo religion. Jesus was making the practice of unconditional and nonviolent love the central characteristic of what it meant to be a follower:

> You have heard that it was said, "An eye for an eye and a tooth for a tooth." But I say to you, Do not resist an evildoer. But if anyone strikes you on the right cheek, turn the other also; and if anyone wants to sue you and take your coat, give your cloak as well; and if anyone forces you to go one mile, go also the second mile. Give to everyone who begs from you, and do not refuse anyone who wants to borrow from you.
>
> You have heard that it was said, "You shall love your neighbor and hate your enemy." But I say to you, Love your enemies and pray for those who persecute you, so that you may be children of your Father in heaven; for he makes his sun rise on the evil and on the good, and sends rain on the righteous and on the unrighteous. For if you love those who love you, what reward do you have? Do not even the tax collectors do the same? And if you greet only your brothers and sisters, what more are you doing than others? Do not even the Gentiles do the same? Be perfect, therefore, as your heavenly Father is perfect. (Matthew 5:38-48)

It was precisely Jesus' message of nonviolent resistance and enemy love that resonated so deeply with Gandhi, providing the foundation for a practical method of resistance and social transformation that came to be known as soul force. Soul force takes the teachings of Jesus seriously and lives them out, quite literally, in the public arena. Gandhi and King both viewed soul force as a spiritual discipline for personal transformation as well as a social strategy for societal change. For King, soul force was his faithful response to Christ's mandate to love his enemy and a non-negotiable quality of Christian discipleship for those he led.

For Christians, soul force is synonymous with the stirring of the kingdom of God within us and the demonstration of the kingdom breaking forth through us. Soul force is vital because it calls us to go beyond mere belief in Jesus to an embodied practice of Christlike love. While Gandhi never claimed to be a Christian in belief, he was a follower of Jesus in the most literal sense. He also encouraged Christians to live more like Jesus if they really wanted to make Christianity more attractive for people of other faiths.[4]

Soul force will require some realignment for many of us. Will we be able to fully embrace ourselves as light bearers who already have access to the source and force of love necessary to change ourselves and our world? Can you imagine how we would live if we truly embraced the reality that *within ourselves*, we have the same access to the power of soul force that Gandhi, King, and others throughout history demonstrated? Can you imagine what life would be like if we really, truly, and consistently embraced this reality and practiced this way of being?

SOUL FORCE MOVES OUTWARD

Soul force is deeply personal and deeply social. While it has been utilized by people of faith in specific social contexts, it is available to all people, in whatever location we find ourselves. Although soul force emanates from within, it doesn't stop until it manifests externally, creating personal, communal, and systemic change. Soul force is not limited to personal spiritual growth alone; it transforms communities and social systems. Soul force creates an outward ripple effect, changing us and changing the world simultaneously.

Soul force is a way of life for courageous and compassionate people. Behind soul force is a theology of love characterized by the strength to love God, our neighbors, and even—and especially—our enemies.[5] Soul force is a deep conviction and trust

4. E. Stanley Jones, *Gandhi: An Interpretation* (Nashville: Abingdon-Cokesbury, 1948), 51.

5. For an in-depth study on King's theology of nonviolence and integration of personal and social transformation, see Martin Luther King Jr., *Strength to Love* (Minneapolis: Fortress Press, 2010). First published 1963.

that, in the words of Martin Luther King, "unarmed truth and unconditional love" are the most potent weapons for transformation in the world.[6] It's an abiding faith that God is on the side of the oppressed and the universe bends toward the cause of justice. Soul force quickens our courage and silences our cynicism. As we align our lives with truth and love and justice, we align with a power greater than ourselves, a power that is unstoppable and enduring.

If a force this strong already lives within each of us, then is it possible that massive change is not really what is required for transformation? What if we only need to effectively harness that which we already possess?

What if we only need to pivot?

THE SEVEN PIVOTS TO COURAGE, COMMUNITY, AND CHANGE

To pivot is to turn or cause to turn in place; to move; to change direction or course.[7] A pivot isn't an entire overhaul. It is a slight directional turn that can open up new possibilities and pathways. We already have greatness inside us, and because we do, we don't need to generate or consume greatness; we simply need to unleash the force within us!

In this book, we introduce seven pivots that can transform your life, organization, community, and world:

- Pivot 1: From fear to freedom
- Pivot 2: From barriers to bridge building
- Pivot 3: From self-centeredness to solidarity
- Pivot 4: From hurt to hope
- Pivot 5: From consuming to creating
- Pivot 6: From charity to change
- Pivot 7: From maintenance to movement

---

6. Martin Luther King Jr., "Acceptance Speech," Nobel Peace Prize, December 10, 1964, Oslo, Norway, https://www.nobelprize.org/nobel_prizes/peace/laureates/1964/king-acceptance_en.html.

7. *American Heritage Roget's Thesaurus* (2013), s.v. "pivot."

Can you imagine what our lives would be like if we each made these seven pivots? Can you imagine how that would affect our organizations? Our communities? Our world? When taken together, these pivots form a mighty movement.

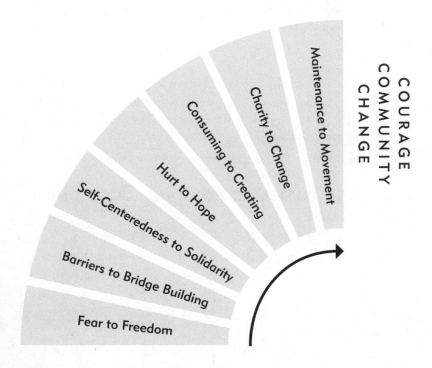

FUEL FOR THE JOURNEY

Soul force is the spiritual energy that makes change happen, and these seven pivots are the small, incremental changes that eventually transform us and those in our communities. Seems so simple, right?

Yet we have been consuming lies about ourselves and our world that have disconnected us from our soul force. And because we lack the energy, we can't do the work required to make the changes. There are messages about our deficits all around us. Messages that tell us:

- We aren't good enough.
- Our dreams are not realistic.

- What we need is outside ourselves and our community.
- Things will never change, and our efforts are hopeless.

But because these messages are lies, we don't need to work harder at disproving them; rather, we simply need to catalyze our soul force. We need to pivot *away* from the lies and change our direction, aligning ourselves, our work, and our communities with what is true:

- We are enough.
- Our dreams are attainable and wilder than we can think or imagine.
- Everything we need lives within us and within our communities.
- Change is possible when we catalyze our soul force.

What would it look like for each of us to resist the false messaging? What would it look like for us to grab hold of the truth: that we are enough, that our dreams are quite attainable, that we have everything we need within ourselves and our communities, and that soul force is the energy that catalyzes the change we want to see in ourselves and in the world?

What would happen if, when we slipped into that old, negative narrative, we began to practice a polite insistence on the truth? What if, instead of beating ourselves up for slipping into negative self-talk, we politely reminded ourselves to hold firmly to the truth of who we are: enough, empowered, abundant, brilliant, and energized by our own soul force?

Practicing *satyagraha* means resisting superimposed false narratives and politely insisting on our own truth and "enoughness." Small incremental changes like this are necessary for a transformational movement to occur both within us and beyond. This is the fundamental power of soul force and why it is so central to the journey we will take in the upcoming chapters: it is literally the energy required to fuel the journey ahead.

We invite you to discover your soul force, to move from the societal shackles that bind to the Spirit who frees. *Soul Force* will develop and deepen your capacity to pivot from lies to liberation and unleash the dormant soul force within you toward courage, community, and change. As you read, you will embark on a journey toward the truths that call out fear for what it is. You will move toward an actionable faith that brings fullness of life to your community and your soul.

THE LIGHT AND THE SHADOW

A word of balance as we embark on this journey. A pivot requires us to turn *away* from one way of being and *toward* something else. In discussing such turns, it is important for us to name that none of the elements which we turn from are innately evil. At times, fear keeps us safe from harm; barriers sometimes do keep danger away; self-care can be preservative and significant; charity can be a form of spiritual discipline; some consumption is inevitably necessary in the creative process; hurt often helps us to grow; and maintenance can be a form of stewardship. It's when we overindulge these characteristics that they create shadows. It's when these elements hide the goodness of courage and community that a pivot is in order.

As we take this journey together, know that we are not encouraging dualistic, either/or thinking. Rather, we are inviting you to expand your vision and exponentialize your freedom, bridge building, solidarity, creativity, hope, and movement toward courage, community, and change.

THE ARC OF THE BOOK

As we mentioned, Jesus, Gandhi, and King all espoused this manner of being—for themselves and for those within the communities in which they led and served. However, soul force is not only reserved for canonical leaders. You don't have to wait until you have acquired a lofty position or formal authority to tap into soul force. Anyone anywhere can lean into soul force as a source of spiritual energy at any time. In fact, many people already are! There are untold stories of maximized soul force all around us.

In this book, we will share some of those stories in the hope that you will see your own potential to live more courageously and be a catalyst for change within your own community. We will also share stories of our own lives and work that illustrate the pivots and the power of soul force.

We are writing as facilitators—as "guides on the side"—rather than as figureheads. As artist-activists rather than topic authorities. Our role is not to give answers or tell you what to do but to help you identify the barriers holding you back from your full potential for change. Both of us are ministers and community leaders who work to bring change from the grass roots to the grass tips. As the executive director of Communities First Association, I (Reesheda) coach leaders in building community and developing sustainable and equitable practices within their organizations. I have had to tap into soul force to launch my dream of L!VE Café, an experiential community space that serves artisanal coffee and brings people from across Chicago together for conversation and mutual transformation.

I (Shawn) serve as the executive director of Mission Year, a national Christian organization that empowers young people to live a lifestyle of love and justice. I have had to tap into soul force as a neighborhood advocate, youth mentor, prison volunteer, and justice activist. We need soul force daily to meet the challenges of our professional and personal lives.

We are both passionate about transformation and motivating people toward movement. We both come from a Christian faith orientation, so those commitments will come through in these pages. But soul force is not limited to only those who claim allegiance to Christian faith. Because soul force is unarmed truth and unconditional love, it is accessible to anyone who aligns themselves with truth and love.

The next seven chapters correspond to the seven pivots and go into greater detail about what each pivot entails. At the end of each chapter, to provide ongoing practices to reinforce each transformational pivot, you'll find a soul force pivot story, pivot application points, and a pivot mantra (prayer). The appendices contain additional resources, including discussion and reflection questions.

Remember, soul force is not something external to who you are; it means aligning your inner core with what is true, practicing purposeful being rather than frantic activity. Soul force means setting the creative force within you free so that you can experience movement within yourself and your community.

A SOUL FORCE PRAYER

This prayer is by Howard Thurman, a minister, theologian, and civil rights activist who was committed to nonviolence and building beloved community. Let this be our prayer and rallying cry as we begin this journey toward soul force.

Lord, open unto me

Open unto me—light for my darkness.

Open unto me—courage for my fear.

Open unto me—hope for my despair.

Open unto me—peace for my turmoil.

Open unto me—joy for my sorrow.

Open unto me—strength for my weakness.

Open unto me—wisdom for my confusion.

Open unto me—forgiveness for my sins.

Open unto me—love for my hates.

Open unto me—thy Self for my self.

Lord, Lord, open unto me!

Amen.[8]

---

8. Howard Thurman, *Meditations of the Heart* (Boston: Beacon Press, 1981), 188.

Pivot 1

FROM FEAR TO FREEDOM

I learned that courage was not the absence of fear, but the triumph over it.

—NELSON MANDELA, *LONG WALK TO FREEDOM*

We cannot be free in any area of our lives until we confront our fears. Fear can be an all-encompassing impediment to transformation for individuals, leaders, and organizations. Fear can be crippling and can keep us from taking risks, both personally and professionally.

Soul force requires courage in the face of fear. If we want to experience movement in our lives, we have to learn to pivot from fear to freedom.

We will discuss explicit ways we can be agents of social change in the following chapters, but we want to start by unmasking a few of the fears and the complications underlying some of the injustices we encounter in our communities. Uprooting fear and exposing the lies makes room for more freedom and justice in the world.

In 2011, I (Reesheda) had the honor of traveling to the Democratic Republic of Congo. Before my arrival, I sought the wise counsel of friends, one of whom was of Nigerian descent. His advice was for me to be open, suspending anything I thought I knew about place, people, and even about myself. This one piece of advice was what left me most receptive to my own opportunity for transformation.

I was in the DRC for almost two weeks, and during that time I heard many fascinating stories and learned to suspend my own assumptions. One experience was more precious to me than the rest, however, as it illuminates how absolutely captivated by fear we often are.

On this occasion I was sitting with twelve women, a collective participating in a microfinance initiative. Each month, each woman would contribute a portion of her savings to a lockbox. At the end of each month, one of those twelve women would inherit the contents of the box, with a few caveats: (1) the woman had to use the funds to either start a business or develop a business that she had already started; and (2) being a part of the collective meant sharing thoughts, ideas, and strategies of business development with one another. This circle of women became an accountability think tank, of sorts.

One of the women told an incredibly inspiring story. She had started out with the purchase of two chickens, using their eggs to both sell to others and feed her family. She went on to discover how to incubate baby chicks to produce more chickens to sell and to feed her family. Finally, this woman went on to develop a workshop through which she taught other people in her village how to do the work she was doing, even with other animals.

I was deeply inspired by the work of this one woman in enhancing her community, and I immediately wondered whether such models of community development—microfinance, small business development, and accountability circles—could exist in areas like the Austin community in Chicago where I spent my childhood years. I was excited by the value such economic development could produce in communities like Austin, as well as the relational fabric that comes as a byproduct of such circles.

Yet right away I also began to consider what might inhibit such a circle in the U.S. context. Who would be trusted to hold the funds? What would happen if someone did not uphold the norms and agreements established by the group? What if someone ran off with the group's money? What if someone's business, despite her best efforts, legitimately failed? Questions overcame my initial hopefulness.

So I started asking the twelve women in the circle these questions. Their eyebrows furrowed and their lips turned on the corners, revealing smirks that should be trademarked to Congolese women. Seeing their faces, I knew that my questions had revealed my "otherness."

The women answered that they had no time, energy, or desire to dispel the concerns I had articulated. Simply put, they had both *nothing* and *everything* to lose. The absence of material wealth left them free from the worries of losing it (nothing). Their desperation to feed and care for their children (everything) urged them toward the hope and possibility inherent in actually *doing something*.

My relative material wealth (in comparison to my Congolese sisters) and my knowledge that my children were safe and comfortable: these very conditions contributed to my inability to take the risks associated with such transformational, communal, relational activity.

Immediately a new question emerged. Would I have to lose everything in order to tap into the love, courage, and strength that these women were sharing with one another? Or was it possible for me to learn from what they had shared and move beyond my own fear?

It was in this moment that I realized that fear had captivated me. Not only that, but it was an unnecessary fear—an unrealistic fear, and one that I had been conditioned to nurture and satiate, to pacify and quell. For forty years, I had learned fear through institutions such as schools, churches, family, and media. But now there was this new question: Could I move from a place of fear to a place of risk, faith, and collective impact?

There is a fine and sometimes indistinct line between the fears that keep us safe and the ones that imprison us. Like amber trapping a firefly, limiting its movement and the magnificence of its shining light, fear snatches away our collective impact. Fear of loss, betrayal, and discomfort paralyzes the gifts that emerge when we are in relationship with one another. But when we relinquish some of our own perceived safety and comfort, we are free to experience life more deeply with others. We become active participants in the transformational power that is unbridled when we overcome our fear.

As I left the twelve wise women of Congo, I knew that I was forever changed. My mindset was different. I have not been completely released from fears, of course; I still have them quite frequently. All the systems that are in place to evoke fear in my life continue to work toward that end. Yet I am now more conscious and aware of those mechanisms and how I respond to them. I can now often move forward *in spite of* the trepidation and uncertainty that challenge me.

This new reality—recognizing and naming fear but not allowing it to rob me of the gifts associated with overcoming it—allows me to live with uncertainty. I hold what I *think* I know more loosely, and I allow my thoughts, my environment, and the people around me to be less defined. It is not always comfortable, and it is not usually predictable. But it is always enriching.

Relentless fears can paralyze us, preventing us from living fully and experiencing freedom, creativity, and joy. The fears that hold us back are often lies that we have internalized from society and people in our lives. Behind every fear is a lie that must be unmasked. Naming our fears is a necessary first step in overcoming them. Our personal, leadership, and societal fears must be addressed if we are to move toward courage, community, and change.

PERSONAL FEARS

Fear of failure, pain, and rejection are some of the inner fears we have to face if we are going to experience personal freedom. When we allow our lives to be driven by fear, we don't take risks, we avoid challenges, and we close ourselves off from others. When we respond inappropriately to fear, we become people-pleasers who assimilate to who we think others want us to be. Freedom, on

1.1 Three examples of personal fears

Fear	Lie	Behavior	Pivot
Failure	"I have to be perfect."	Don't take risks; live in shame	Take risks, and give room to fail
Pain	"This pain will last forever."	Avoid challenges	Do hard things, knowing pain is temporary
Rejection	"No one will accept me as I am."	Close yourself off; become a people-pleaser	Open yourself up to others, letting them see the real you

the other hand, is the courage to be ourselves fully. Rather than living out lies, we can embrace the truth about ourselves and live in fuller freedom.

Those of us who fear failure and internalize the lie of perfectionism must learn the truth that we are all broken. By acknowledging our brokenness and embracing our imperfect selves, we free ourselves from the burden of being perfect. We give ourselves grace and allow ourselves room to fail.

As a recovering perfectionist, I (Shawn) lived in constant fear of failure. When I didn't live up to the ideals of myself or my faith, I experienced heavy guilt and shame. This fear of failure led me to hide my imperfections and present the parts of me I wanted the world to see. In college, during a confession service in which the student body was invited to publicly confess our deepest failures, I finally grasped the concept of God's grace. I sat glued to my seat for hours as I watched other students approach the front of the auditorium, openly confess their deep brokenness, and then experience the freedom of grace from God and one another.

I wanted that freedom so desperately, but I also feared being exposed. What would people think of me? Finally, I decided that moving toward freedom was worth the risk, and I pivoted out of my seat and walked down to the front.

The freedom I felt from unloading the shame of failure was unbelievable. All of a sudden I understood what grace meant. I realized that I was broken like everyone else, and that God loved me, even in my brokenness. This transformed my relationship with

God and opened the door for freedom in many areas of my life. I learned I can live in fear and shame, or I can embrace grace and live free.

Are you living timidly because you are afraid of making mistakes? What would you attempt if you weren't afraid of failing?

LEADERSHIP FEARS

We are both leaders of national organizations, and as such, we have the opportunity to mentor and coach emerging leaders. Fear of inadequacy, vulnerability, and scarcity are common leadership fears we encounter. These are fears most leaders wrestle with on a weekly, sometimes daily basis!

Fear of inadequacy is especially prevalent for those taking on a new leadership role. Most transformational leaders we know have felt inadequate. In fact, if you *didn't* feel inadequate when you are stepping into leadership, we would be worried. As they say, pride comes before the fall. But while a sense of inadequacy may be perfectly normal, dwelling in that emotion such that it becomes the place from which you live and lead can also hold a leader back.

We know a nonprofit leader who is constantly berating himself. He is crippled by feelings of inadequacy and self-doubt. He constantly needs reassurance from those he leads, and he is reluctant to lead on crucial matters. He is in desperate need of a pivot. Leaders must learn to trust themselves and the gifts God has given them. Trusting yourself doesn't mean you are always

1.2 Three examples of leadership fears

Fear	Lie	Behavior	Pivot
Inadequacy	"I am not good enough."	Live in self-doubt, with a reluctance to lead	Trust yourself and be confident in your gifts
Vulnerability	"I have to appear strong."	Hide weaknesses	Admit mistakes and practice vulnerability
Scarcity	"There aren't enough resources."	Hold on to a competitive spirit, and even hopelessness	Cultivate a cooperative spirit and creativity

right; it simply means believing that you are capable of making good decisions and being willing to take responsibility for those decisions. Sometimes you trust yourself and you end up making a bad decision. That is where humility becomes crucial. Being confident in your gifts doesn't mean being arrogant. Apologize for the mistakes you make when leading, but don't apologize for leading.

Many leaders also have a fear of being vulnerable. Leaders are often put on pedestals, which makes it hard to confess vulnerability. They may have supervisors or board members who scrutinize their work, so they feel that they can't show any sign of weakness. But when leaders operate out of fear, they don't operate as their best or most true selves. They end up living out false narratives and keeping others from living freely as well. Vulnerability frees leaders to be human, to admit mistakes, and to show others their authentic selves. Vulnerable leaders elicit trust in their followers and create spaces where others can be vulnerable as well. Henri Nouwen said it best: "We are called to be fruitful—not successful, not productive, not accomplished. Success comes from strength, stress, and human effort. Fruitfulness comes from vulnerability and the admission of our own weakness."[1]

I (Shawn) went to a workshop at a leadership gathering in Atlanta, and one of the leaders of the local L'Arche community shared on the topic of vulnerability in our stories. He told us the founding story of the L'Arche community. The story goes that Jean Vanier felt a call to start an intentional community in which people with and without disabilities live, work, and worship together. He took two young men to France to start the community, which grew into an international movement. L'Arche communities are now found in hundreds of cities across the world.

But what was missing from this rather well-know version of the story, the leader confessed to us, was that Vanier actually took three men to France. One of the young men had such severe problems that the others couldn't help him, and they had to send him home. This part of the story is not usually told, he said. The

---

1. Quoted in Johann Christoph Arnold, *Seeking Peace: Notes and Conversations along the Way* (New York: Plume, 2000), 54.

temptation for us as leaders and ministers is to hide the vulnerability in our stories—to leave out the parts of our stories that we're
afraid of revealing.

I was instantly convicted. I thought back on times I had tried to
protect myself and my organization from being vulnerable: high-
lighting only the good aspects, diverting board members' attention
away from what wasn't working well, or only posting my successes on social media and not my struggles.

Brené Brown, the guru of vulnerability, describes the struggle
and joy of being vulnerable in her book *The Gifts of Imperfection*: "Owning our story can be hard but not nearly as difficult as
spending our lives running from it. Embracing our vulnerabilities
is risky, but not nearly as dangerous as giving up on love, belonging, and joy—the experiences that make us the most vulnerable.
Only when we are brave enough to explore the darkness will we
discover the infinite power of our light."[2]

Scarcity is another common fear for those in leadership, especially those who are operating organizations with limited budgets
and resources. It's amazing how quickly our minds jump from
scarcity to "doomsday" scenarios. As organizational leaders, both
of us are familiar with those feelings of dread related to having
limited funding. Operating from a place of scarcity often invokes
hopelessness or a competitive spirit. All of a sudden we see others
in our field as competitors rather than potential collaborators.

But having limited resources does not mean our organization
or dream is over. Remember the Congolese women in the beginning of the chapter? They had limited resources, but they didn't
operate from a mentality of scarcity. As a result, they unleashed a
cooperative and creative spirit.

Both of us work in Chicago, and we are both responsible for
raising money to keep each of our organizations going. We could
have chosen to see each other as competitors, each of us jostling
for scarce funding from donors and organizations. But instead
of being competitive, we decided to pivot and work together

---

2. Brené Brown, *The Gifts of Imperfection: Let Go of Who You Think You're Supposed to Be and Embrace Who You Are* (Center City, MN: Hazelden, 2010), 6.

cooperatively. We serve on each other's boards, we share grant opportunities and donors, and we do events together.

Making this shift has given us both life, and it has helped sustain our organizations at the same time. What if this type of collaboration became the norm with churches, organizations, and businesses?

SOCIETAL FEARS

The last set of fears we want to explore in this chapter are societal fears. Societal fears include the fear of those who are different from us, the fear of being prejudged by others, and the fear of losing privilege, comfort, and security. These fears can not only impede personal growth; they can perpetuate oppressive social conditions in our communities and world.

Fear of those who are different is rampant in society. Culture, media, and politics often incite fears of those who look, believe, vote, speak, or live differently. These fears can lead people to retreat into isolation; as a result, ignorance, which enables prejudice and oppression, takes root. This destructive spiral incites an "us versus them" mentality. There's a saying: "We don't fear people whose story we know." When we don't know each other's stories, it's easier to demonize and dehumanize others. Fear of difference is at the root of so many social injustices: the removal and extermination of Native Americans, the enslavement of African Americans, the

1.3 Three examples of societal fears

Fear	Lie	Behavior	Pivot
Others who are different	"We have nothing in common."	Live in isolation, ignorance, prejudice, and oppression	Build bridges of relationship to listen, learn, and understand
Being prejudged by others	"We are what others perceive us to be."	Dwell in frustration, anxiety, and self-hatred	Be unapologetically you, offering your gifts to the world
Losing privilege, comfort, and security	"Some deserve more than others; life is a zero-sum game."	Be defensive and hostile, and internalize dominance and inequity	Commit to work for justice, and be willing to sacrifice for the greater good

imprisonment of Japanese Americans in internment camps, and current examples of mass incarceration and aggressive immigration policies. Unmasking these fears and intentionally choosing closer proximity with people who are different from us allows us to challenge stereotypes and expose prejudice.

Before I (Shawn) moved to Chicago, I had many fears about urban neighborhoods. As a white person, I believed the cultural lie that people of color living in inner-city communities were so different from me that we would not be able to develop deep bonds of relationship. I had internalized messages that urban communities were dangerous, and that if I wanted to be safe, I had better stay out. The media had given me a very one-sided narrative of the city, so all I knew were the stories of violence. When I learned about the injustice in the city and felt a call to move closer, I had to wrestle with the tension between my fear of others and my desire to live in deep relationship and freedom with those who were different from me. My wife and I finally decided to make the move, but I still felt a lot of anxiety about the perceived and real threats of violence that plagued our neighborhood.

Linda, one of the neighbors I met early on, told me about her own anxieties and how her faith helped her to choose love over fear. She taught me that I do not have to be ruled by fear, and that faith is not the absence of fear, but the courage to trust despite our fears. I have learned that it's hard to fear others when you love them, and it's hard to love others when you fear them. Love does indeed drive out fear.

So many of my fears have been vanquished as I have entered into relationship with people in the neighborhood. In fact, I have learned what soul force looks like by watching their authenticity, resilience, and courage in the face of overwhelming trauma and injustice. Had I allowed my fears to rule over me, I would have missed out on some great relationships, as well as a journey of transformation that has helped me come alive in so many areas of my life.

Many of us have probably experienced the fear of being judged by others, whether it's for outward appearances such as height, weight, or how we dress or for abilities we have or don't have. But those who come from social locations that have been historically denied access and power often feel the sting even more severely. Our society is far from Martin Luther King's dream of being judged not by our color but by our character. The burden of being the only person of color or woman in the boardroom can be a heavy burden to bear and can create a lot of anxiety and self-doubt.

Additionally, those who come from social locations of access and power—whether racial, economic, or otherwise—often fear losing the privilege, comfort, or security they have known. For a person who has privilege and fears losing it, any movement toward equity can be perceived as a threat. This can foster defensiveness, resentment, and even hostility toward those who are advocating for equity. We see this in some negative attitudes toward America's growing diversity, and in the hostility toward immigrants and refugees in countries across the world.

To complicate matters, many who have historically been judged deficient—and continue to be judged so on the basis of race, class, or gender—have experienced *some* access, although usually not to the same extent that their white male counterparts have. This moderate access to power and wealth, combined with popular culture's messages of inadequacy, can lead to a duality of fear. For example, a professional woman of color may be fearful both of being marginalized because of her race and gender *and* of losing the measure of power or privilege that she has gained. This "dual fear dynamic" can be more debilitating than having one or the other—access or no access—in that it breeds pendulum-like behavior. Someone in this position may go back and forth between internalizing self-hatred—a self-hatred that stems from having heard her entire life that she is never enough—and abandoning her community and cultural identity in an effort to win and maintain status in the dominant culture.

Those coming from positions of access and power because of racial, economic, and gender privilege may hold a dual fear dynamic as well. White people may fear being prejudged as ignorant, uncaring, or racist for being white and holding racial privilege while simultaneously fearing the prospect of relinquishing those privileges or making sacrifices to create a greater equality. This dual fear can cause people to stay silent in order to avoid saying the wrong thing. Unfortunately, this ends up preserving the status quo and maintaining privilege. It can be scary to challenge a system from which you are benefiting, and speaking out against it can alienate you from those in your family and social networks. It's also possible for white people to swing between 1) defensiveness and denial of privilege and 2) an internalized self-hatred for being a beneficiary of an institutional system of advantage. Both of these responses prevent the flourishing of true freedom and community between those with access and power and those without. The goal is not to feel guilty about privilege but to work for justice in partnership with those without access and power to ensure that all the institutions of society are truly serving everyone.

Creating a more diverse and equitable world requires sacrifices, but these sacrifices for the greater good bring freedom to both those who have been denied access and those who have held power. It's not a zero-sum game. Our freedom is actually bound up together.

BE COURAGEOUS: A PIVOT TO FREEDOM

Soul force both requires and builds our capacity for courage. Courage is not the absence of fear but the decision to step out despite fear. Courageous leaders are desperately needed in our world. Courage has more to do with faithfulness in the small decisions of everyday life, however, than it does with the monumental decisions that mark a life of distinction. When we confront the small fears of life, we quickly realize that most fears are irrational obstacles stacked up against living a life of true significance. What makes someone a transformational leader is a willingness to face fears and take small steps of faith, *over and over and over and over.*

In 2017, I (Reesheda) had the amazing experience of opening L!VE, a transformational experience café. This boutique coffeehouse, with intentional coffee, intentional community, and intentional space, offers transformation by supporting local suppliers, training and coaching staff in entrepreneurship, and gathering people together for conversation and events like poverty simulations. Now I have the joy of watching community unfold between people who otherwise may never have met or connected with one another. I am seeing the rewards of having launched out and taken risks.

Yet I did not always possess the courage necessary to pursue what had, in essence, been a lifelong goal. Frankly, I was terrified of this vision. While it was so unmistakably clear in my head—that I was to create this hub that allowed community-minded folks to come together—all the details seemed unanswerable and left me debilitated.

As a Black, middle-class woman who looks young (and therefore inexperienced), I was plagued by memories of racism, misogyny, classism, and adultism (age-related bias against young people). I began to doubt my ability to pull the venture off successfully. Would banks, with their inequitable lending practices toward traditionally marginalized people groups, keep me from acquiring a loan? Would I succumb to the predatory lending options available to people like me who want to start a business? Would I be duped by the systems that intentionally never teach people who look and sound like me the skill sets required to be an effective entrepreneur? Would I be disrespected and ignored as a woman working to start a business? Would my youthful looks actually serve as a barrier to people taking me seriously? (Although I am forty-two years old, many people assume I am in my twenties, and people have sometimes judged my capacity on the basis of this assumption.)

All these questions were hanging in the balance, even while I was also considering the fears associated with the potential loss of status, material wealth, comfort, and security that come with being educated and holding a relative position of power. What would happen to my current position as the executive director of Communities First Association and the financial security that came with holding that position? Could I lose my house, the place

where my family lives and finds comfort? If this failed, would I
no longer be seen as a dynamic community leader? Would people
still ask me to write, speak, and lead on topics related to Christian
community development?

The last two fears in this section—fear of being judged for things
like race, class, and gender, and fear of losing privilege, comfort,
and security—were running amok inside me. And because they
were, I could not make the larger move from fear to freedom without the smaller change: the pivot.

Here was the pivot that I chose: I decided that despite all the
fears I was feeling, I simply wanted to carry out the vision of L!VE
more than I wanted my fears to rule over me. I decided that while
I was still afraid of all the details and questions and how they
would be answered and carried out in my life, I was going to move
forward with the vision anyway. It is important to note that I had
no new information about any of the questions that gave me pause
and worry. I had no new insights on how "isms" would affect
my process, no new insights on how much comfort and security
would be at stake if I decided to move forward. And I was still
afraid of and grappling with all the same questions and worries
that were crippling my efforts.

The pivot was me simply deciding to *do it anyway*. The pivot
was trusting that, by faith, I was intended to do this work. I courageously committed to stay the course, come what may, recognizing
that the journey to carrying out the vision was more valuable, even
with bumps in the road, than sitting still. Get this: the courage
to let go of the outcome allows us to pivot from both the actual
and perceived fears associated with the "what-ifs" and to move
toward the freedom associated with courageous, authentic, and
abundant living!

Choosing courage is not easy. But as soon as I chose to live
courageously, a sense of freedom pervaded each step. I was no
longer operating "underneath" my fears. I still thought about systemic injustice and was aware of my feelings about it; I just didn't
craft my plans as one who had to acquiesce to it. Once I pivoted
toward courage and freedom, I trusted in the vision I was called to,

and I carried out decisions and plans that were in alignment with freedom rather than with fear.

And did those isms—racism, misogyny, classism, and adult-ism—play out in the process? Absolutely! Did I see isms for what they were? Sure I did. But living from a place of freedom, I responded to them very differently than I would have responded had I been living from a place of fear. I was more prophetic in how I named the presence of isms when they showed up. Rather than attempting to avoid them and their aftermath, I gave the ism purveyors—both individuals and organizations—an opportunity to see their implicit and explicit participation in systems that sub-jugate and oppress. As one who carries a moderate amount of privilege and access, I was relinquishing my security as a member of the protected people group called the "educated middle class" to stand in solidarity with people who look and sound like me but who lack the access I have.

I was *aware* of my fear of being uncomfortable, but I disengaged my fear enough to engage freedom—not only on behalf of myself but also on behalf of a collective that has been disenfranchised and disinherited. In choosing to pivot toward freedom and away from fear, I unleashed soul force. I raised my voice on behalf of justice and equity, and the impact of this choice has outweighed what my small vision would have been able to do on its own. Artists and entrepreneurs who had never had an opportunity to share their gifts and talents now sell their products in the café. Women who had not been afforded opportunities to lead now manage the café. Groups who have had disagreements in virtual spaces have come together face-to-face to practice reconciliation in the café. And the space is becoming known as the place to go to have community conversations and to conspire toward activism. This is how the pivot leads to the movement!

Because fear is at the root of so many of the lies we believe about ourselves and the world, the first pivot may be the most significant of them all. Pivoting from a life of fear into a life of freedom has a ripple effect on our entire lives. The pivot from fear to freedom clears the way for future pivots.

Before moving on, take some time to reflect on the fears that are impediments to freedom for you and your community. What movements could you make to unleash greater freedom and courage?

SOUL FORCE STORY

From fear to freedom

Gabriel Lam

Before I begin to tell my story about finding freedom in the midst of fear, I need you to understand why it has taken me thirty years to write, and why I still write under a pseudonym. In order to understand that, you'll need a few biographical details about me: (1) I grew up in multiple Asian countries (which are much more conservative than the United States); (2) I received an American education in those Asian countries; (3) I grew up in a fundamentalist Christian household; and (4) I identify as gay.

It has taken me thirty years to write because I was born into this no-man's-land between violently warring worlds, each one bloodthirsty for my allegiance against the others: East versus West, gay versus straight, conservative versus liberal. I knew that if I didn't play by these rules, I would be cut off from community.

Maybe it's hard for you to imagine if you're reading this from the West, but being cut off from community is existential death. So I grew up afraid. Afraid of not fully belonging under any sacred canopy. Afraid that fully belonging in one tribe meant having to cut off parts of myself that felt more essential than my legs, or my arms, or my sight. So I chose the other option: I chose to not ever fully belong, I chose to live with memberships in secret, and also to live in perpetual fear. I opted for the art of code-switching—that is, the art of deceit—for the sake of survival. And while I still feel the devastating effects of this choice, on my good days I think this was the right choice for me.

But life has a way of squeezing you into choosing between further integration or disintegration. In my twenties, I began to come out to friends, and overall it was a good experience. But quickly, the new battle lines came into clear focus. From one side I heard, "Will you be a faithful, Bible-believing Christian? Or will you be a flaming liberal who doesn't care about God's Word and will eventually burn in hell?" From the other side I heard, "Will you stand with Jesus, with the oppressed and the marginal? Or will you be an oppressive, bigoted, self-hating conservative who doesn't care about his own people and doesn't take Jesus' words seriously?"

An unlikely host of folks gave me a third way through the violence: Black Lives Matter, Dr. King, Howard Thurman, Gandhi, and Jesus gave me a way through the violence, through the fear of death. As I sat at the feet of crying mothers, as I joined Black folks in America protesting police brutality, as I read sermons, speeches, and stories, I relearned the Sermon on the Mount, the kingdom of God, and learned the power of facing the violence straight on through love, the power of nonviolent resistance.

The reality is that I cannot outrun the violence. And further, my running both feeds the fear and stirs it into a frenzy. But what I can do instead is to stop and turn, like countless bodies have before me, and choose to stand: vulnerable and weak, truly human, killable. So I choose to stand with the vulnerable Jesus, who embraced death, not scorning but absorbing the violence, and who triumphed over Hades; and whose voice echoes through the ages: "Those who lose their life for my sake will find it" (Matthew 16:25).

So I stand as fully me: fearful, but no longer running, no longer lying, and finally beginning to make peace with myself. I choose simply to live publicly in between, in the no-man's-land. I choose to make peace with being undecided on "the gay issue," knowing that this will cause both left and right to weaponize against me. I can't blame them, but I also can no longer lie. I now understand that violence comes from fear; and as I've understood the fear, I no longer am afraid of the violence it produces. Fear drives us to violently eliminate so that we can survive. Who can blame us? I deeply empathize with the survival mentality. But this mentality ends in a death worse than death.

So this is my story. It continues to unfold. Each day I am learning a bit more how to love myself and others, to humanize, and to absorb violence. Each day I'm practicing a bit more how to die instead of how to lie, run, and cut off in fear.

I can understand how my story might ring a little hollow, as I write "openly" but under a pseudonym. This paradox (of writing about fear and freedom while still under a guise) should invite critique, and hopefully charity. I have chosen to write under a pseudonym to honor my family and the collective communities they belong to in Asia. I hope that this small death of transparency does not subtract too greatly from the words I have penned but rather invites you to stand with me in the liminal space between our warring worlds. Peace to you, dear friend; might we find life!

SOUL FORCE PIVOT POINTS

The following are pivot points: questions and exercises intended to guide you toward personal reflection and action. Our hope is that these pivot points can unearth deep fears, mobilize your soul force, and move you into greater freedom.

Name the fears

What fears have been ingrained in you? How did they get there? What role have familial, cultural, religious, societal, academic, or political connections played in the creation of your fears, albeit intentionally or unintentionally? What role have the media and communications and the use of technology and social media played in the creation or conflagration of your fears?

Choose one fear. Peel back the layers as far as you can of how it came to be, how it still exists within you, and how it plays out in your life. How has it helped you? How has it harmed you? How has it debilitated you? What would happen if you disengaged it?

Take baby steps to face your fears

What are some small ways you can live in the truth? How might you pivot toward courage and move from fear to freedom in your everyday life?

Find people who seem to lead a less fearful life, and learn from them

Who are some people you know who are living freedom over fear? What do you witness in them? What might you embody in your own life as a result of what you learn from them?

Never allow fear to cause you to dehumanize another

What people or places are you afraid of? How can you move into closer proximity to them in order to hear their stories? What about those people or places do you also see in yourself? Are there any commonalities? What do you share?

PIVOT 1 MANTRA

I choose freedom over fear.

(The mantras: a mantra is a word or phrase that can be repeated as we pray or meditate. Each chapter's pivot will include a mantra to root us in truth and tap into our inner soul force.)

Pivot 2

FROM BARRIERS TO BRIDGE BUILDING

In times of crisis, the wise build bridges, while the foolish build barriers.
—KING T'CHALLA, *BLACK PANTHER* FILM

Humans are gifted at erecting walls, defining borders, and building barriers. Sometimes these barriers and boundaries serve us well, keeping us safe from danger and harm. Indeed, healthy barriers sometimes need to be constructed. When we overuse barriers, however, we can make safety into an idol, destroy relationships, and prevent ourselves from learning and growing. Barriers, when erected out of fear, create dividing walls between people that prevent interaction and mutual understanding.

In October 2014, Laquan McDonald, a ward of the state with a history of neglect and abuse by those closest to him, had wandered the Chicago streets aimlessly, allegedly holding a knife and puncturing car tires. Within seconds of arriving on the scene, white police officer Jason Van Dyke opened fire on McDonald, who was Black, shooting him sixteen times. A reporter sued the city for the release of the dashboard camera video and uncovered a $5 million settlement payment that had been made from the city to the family in exchange for their silence.[1] The mayor denied ever seeing the video.

Upon the release of the video one year after the incident, thousands of protesters, including church members and college students, converged on Michigan Avenue. The protest shut down Chicago's highest profile shopping district on Black Friday, one of the busiest shopping days of the year. Protesters counted in unison from one to sixteen, to mark every bullet that went into McDonald's body. Crowds cried out for the firing of state's attorney Anita Alvarez, who was voted out in the next election cycle. Soon after the release of the video, the mayor terminated the police chief, either in response to this public outcry or possibly to save himself.

During the year between when McDonald was killed and when the video was released, a strong divide emerged: between communities of color and police, between urban and suburban areas, and between white churches and churches primarily composed of people of color. In response to numerous Black Lives Matter protests, Blue Lives Matter had begun to rise as a counter rallying cry. The mounting tension between police and communities of color led many residents to stop calling the police and had caused some police to stop responding to calls. Some activists had begun taking a more extreme and oppositional approach, even shouting out, in the words of the hip-hop group N.W.A., "F—— the police!"

One night we both attended a prayer vigil hosted by faith leaders in the city to commemorate the anniversary of the shooting of Laquan McDonald. As we made our way to the police headquarters on the South Side of Chicago, we knew that tensions would be high. News camera trucks lined the street. The media seemed eager to hear what kind of response the faith community would have in a moment like this. Pastors huddled around the microphone in the middle of the large crowd. Protest chants filled the air. This prayer vigil didn't start out sounding much different from other protests

---

1. Kyung Lah, "Laquan McDonald Shooting: Why Did It Take 13 Months to Release Video?," CNN News, December 2, 2015, http://www.cnn.com/2015/12/01/us/chicago-police-shooting-explainer/index.html.

happening across the city. The first couple of speakers took an aggressive tone, and a clear physical division took shape between the faith community and the police who were lined up outside the police station.

Reesheda and I (Shawn) found each other in the crowd, and we discovered that we were feeling a similar uneasiness about what we were witnessing. We were uncomfortable with the chasm between the police and the community of faith. Reesheda mentioned how her faith calls her to question any marginalization, since marginalization is often at the root of injustice and oppression. I felt stirred in my spirit to bridge the divide too, but I felt reluctant to do something by myself.

I turned to Reesheda and nodded toward the line of police officers standing outside the station. "If you want to go over there, I'll go with you," I said. She agreed, and we left the circle of the praying faithful and took steps across the divide.

Walking the ten or fifteen feet that separated the two sides, we approached two police officers. We told them we were interested in talking with them to see how they were feeling about being on the outside of this prayer circle.

"Black-on-Black crime happens every day," one officer said to us. "Where's the outrage then? Why aren't you out there protesting that?" I told him that a lot of us live in communities where violence is happening, and we are constantly working on addressing it. "The problem is, there's a system of accountability in place when Black youth commit a crime," I said, "but there's no similar system of accountability for police."

That seemed to be a point he hadn't considered before. The conversation was cordial. The officers told us that they were not the enemy. We talked about ways the police and community could work together. One African American female officer talked about how she was actively involved in her church and community. Reesheda exchanged contact information with her, and we let the officers know we were praying for them as well as our communities.

We left the vigil feeling conflicted. What does it really mean to be people of faith in the midst of deep division? Do we have a unique role and responsibility? Can we stand with the marginalized without marginalizing those who don't agree with our stance? How can we hear our opponents rather than further isolating them? After the vigil, we wondered what it would have looked like if one of the police officers had been invited to offer a prayer at the vigil.

In our lives and in our work, are we creating barriers or are we creating bridges?

In order to build sound bridges, we must first address the barriers. When fear and a desire for security go unchecked, barriers marginalize and dehumanize others. When barriers endure, healthy communication and human connection can be lost. Nowhere is this more obvious than in our current political climate. In order to hear one another and work together for the common good, we will need to deconstruct the barriers keeping us divided.

FOUR DUALITIES OF BARRIERS

We have identified four dualities in which we create and construct barriers: internal and external, conscious and unconscious, individual and collective, and indigenous and institutional. These four dualities often overlap and interplay. Again, none of these constructs are inherently evil or negative. But when we create barriers from unhealthy places of fear, they stand to deplete flourishing.

Internal and external barriers

Internal barriers are not tangible, but they nonetheless serve as dividers between us and those we consider to be "other." An internal barrier could be inner prejudice, unresolved anger, crippling anxiety, depression, or apathy.

2.1 Barriers: Four dualities

Internal / External	Conscious / Unconscious
Individual / Collective	Indigenous / Institutional

As a Black woman in America, I (Reesheda) have had many labels superimposed upon me. Being labeled as "angry" is one of the most significant (not to exclude "strong," "maternal," and "sacrificial"). While I likely do embody these characteristics at times, people call me these things so frequently that I begin to wonder whether, in their minds, these are the only ways I am allowed to be. Being labeled with these attributes has caused feelings of anxiety, depression, and even hopelessness in me. Labels, even positive ones and ones intended as compliments, can become an albatross about my neck.[2]

At times I have likely embodied the lie that all I am capable of being is "an angry Black woman" or even a "strong Black woman." In these moments, I am more prone to build internal barriers between myself and those who have presupposed these labels. Sometimes, in an effort to protect myself, I have closed myself off, creating a barrier between myself and others. At times I have become self-deprecating and emotionally unavailable to those outside a small circle of trusted friends. To be clear, this does not create a more joyful experience for me. More often than not, internal barriers do not create a wider, fuller existence for any of us.

As we discussed in chapter 1, fear can cause us to build barriers between people and ourselves. Once the internal barriers have taken root in our hearts, it's not long before we construct physical barriers.

External barriers are tangible, physical walls, fences, bars, and barricades. History is full of walls. The Berlin Wall, a physical and ideological barrier, divided East and West Germany for thirty years. Established out of fear of fascism and immigration of Europeans from East Germany to West Germany, the wall served as a mechanism of control and imprisonment. The Israeli West Bank wall is another barrier. The Israelis insist it is a security barrier against terrorism, while the Palestinians experience it as an apartheid wall,

---

2. For more on the ways that society burdens Black women and perpetuates the stereotype of the strong Black woman, see Chanequa Walker-Barnes, *Too Heavy a Yoke: Black Women and the Burden of Strength* (Eugene, OR: Cascade, 2014).

maintaining racial segregation. How a physical barrier is experienced often depends on what side of the wall you are on.

Prison is another example of barriers that keep others at a distance. I (Shawn) remember my first visit to a maximum-security prison. First, I noticed how far out in the country it was. Then I noticed the tall, imposing walls as I drove up the long driveway. Barbed wire lined the tops of the walls. I passed through several heavily guarded checkpoints before even getting inside the actual prison. Then I walked long corridors, past more security doors, before arriving at the cell house. When I entered the cell house, I looked up to see five stories of prison cells. Each small cell had thick metal bars restricting the movements and freedom of the two humans forced to reside there.

Physical barriers can be intimidating. But crossing them can be a liberating experience for us and others. One time I took a group of Mission Year volunteers to visit the prison. They had been reading Michelle Alexander's *The New Jim Crow* and talking about mass incarceration, but there's nothing like experiencing prison up close. I talked the prison chaplain into letting a group of women visit the men's prison with me, and we were given clearance to go into the cell houses and interact with some of the men I had gotten to know.

One powerful moment was when Emily, a conservative Christian who had moved to Chicago from Texas, went to visit Eddie's cell. She'd grown up believing people in prison were bad people with whom she had little in common. She went into the prison thinking she might be able to evangelize or give hope to the men inside. But Eddie spent most of the time witnessing to her. He told her what he was learning from Scripture and also shared vulnerably what he was struggling with. At the end, we reached our hands through the bars of the cell and prayed together. By the end of the prayer, Emily was in tears.

When we were back outside, I asked Emily what was going on inside her. She said, "I had certain ideas about people in prison. But when we were praying with Eddie, I realized he's my brother." Barriers keep us from seeing that people we fear and avoid are actually our brothers and sisters.

Conscious and unconscious barriers

So there are the intangible barriers that live within us, and tangible ones, like walls and gates, that are external. Now let's consider the barriers that we are aware of and the ones that we are not. How we interact with these conscious and unconscious barriers will affect our ability to live courageously.

It is not an infrequent occurrence for me (Reesheda) to receive invitations to speak, write, and collaborate with people—specifically with white men—in which my work is requested without an offer of any compensation for my time, expertise, and efforts. Having had this experience more times than I can count, I am now keenly aware of the number of requests I receive, how many I am willing to accept, and under what circumstances. As a rule, unless I have a close relationship with the person making the request, I point out that people of color and women are frequently asked to extend their expertise for free, and the implicit devaluating of their labor that accompanies such requests. In this instance, I am demarcating a *conscious* boundary, one that is healthy for my life and livelihood, in an effort to avoid exploitation and the co-opting of my ideas. This is an example of a conscious and healthy barrier.

Additionally, though, the threat of this sort of misappropriation led, without my knowing, to a paranoia on my part. I began resenting requests by white-led institutions for my collaboration and participation. Without always realizing it, I began "dressing down" those who made the requests, scrutinizing them for evidence of inequity or attempts at manipulation. It took trusted friends to point out this behavior to me. In this instance, I was exhibiting an *unconscious* barrier that had been constructed over time—a barrier of which I was not cognizant.

On this journey toward courageous living, it will be critical for us to be honest with ourselves and allow trusted accountability partners to hold up the proverbial mirror for us. It is critical that we examine those parts of ourselves that we are unable to see on our own. If we are open to receiving feedback, trusted members of our communities can offer us the gift of revelation for that which we are unable to identify alone.

Individual and collective barriers

While we build barriers knowingly (consciously) and unknowingly (unconsciously), we also build them individually, toward our own preservation, and against a collective group. Our individual identity often informs what kinds of barriers we build, and often dictates whom we will build them against, in an effort to protect our singular agenda and the things we want to protect.

For example, individuals who "make it out" of difficult socioeconomic circumstances sometimes attribute their "success" to their hard work and commitment. In doing so, they distance themselves from their former neighbors and friends, citing that they do not want to regress, or that they don't want the things or people they now value to be ill-affected by the circumstances that exist in their former neighborhood or culture. In an effort to protect their individual interests, they build a barrier between themselves and the collectives of which they used to be a part. This can be seen in the dynamic of what is now often referred to as the "commuter church." Thanks to newly acquired socioeconomic status, individuals who used to live in traditionally underserved neighborhoods move out of those neighborhoods. But because of the faith ties they still have with their church, they will drive in to the neighborhood to attend church. Outside of that weekly visit, however, they have relinquished any other ties to the collective who lives there. These kinds of barriers negatively affect the collective, as the resources and talents of the individuals that could be of help and support are withheld from the community.

While these kinds of barriers between individuals and others are damaging to the collective, we do want to recognize that there are times when preserving the individual from a toxic environment is also necessary. Indeed, not all individual barriers are detrimental. Healthy boundaries can be liberating and protect us from mistreatment. When I (Shawn) discovered the concept of boundaries in my twenties, I felt as if I had found the Holy Grail. As a compassionate soul and a pastor's kid, I had minimal boundaries in my life. This manifested in an inability to say no, a fear of disappointing or hurting people, and a bad case of people-pleasing. Growing up, I hadn't felt I had the right to object to or set a boundary with people.

This came to a head for me in college when a male spiritual mentor, in a moment of enthusiasm, pushed me down on the ground during a group meeting and momentarily lay on top of me. It happened before I had time to object, and it was over in a matter of seconds. But it had been enough to make me uncomfortable. Internally, I felt my boundaries were violated, but I had not learned how, nor had the freedom, to express my disapproval. After further reflection and talking with a counselor, I knew I had to confront this leader and tell him that his actions had crossed a line for me, and that I needed him to respect my boundaries. This was incredibly hard for a college sophomore to do. But after I got over the fear of hurting him and spoke the words, he understood and apologized, and I felt empowered. I had set a healthy boundary and stood up for myself. Healthy boundaries are important and are part of emotional maturity and positive self-care. Shifting from barriers to bridge building does not mean having no boundaries; it means having healthy boundaries and removing unhealthy barriers.

Collective barriers also exist, and they pose threats to individuals who do not belong to the collective or who fail to conform. An example of a collective barrier might be "the old boys' network" that exists in many social and business sectors among senior male members from the same social strata. It can be nearly impossible for those on the outside to break in, which can create barriers to employment, funding, or promotions. The challenge of breaking down barriers that are built collectively is that they cannot be torn down alone. It will require most, if not all, of the people associated with the building of the barrier to participate in the dismantling of it. And the truth is that things that are built together tend to last longer; this also applies to barriers and boundaries that are built institutionally.

Indigenous and institutional barriers
Indigenous and institutional barriers are often derived from hierarchical power structures. An agency, wishing to protect its

own interests and relevance, ironically neglects to invite the voice and participation of the community it is intended to serve. These barriers are often developed to preserve the institution's material assets, power, or wealth. Members of the institution often become more interested in the preservation of their mission or goal than they are in the preservation of the dignity of the local community they were intended to serve. The institution sometimes becomes more driven by metrics, data, and outcomes than it is by the expressed needs of the community and the agenda that the community has set. When barriers are implemented by the institution, *against* the community, it denigrates the community's ability to care for themselves, stripping them of their dignity and humanity.

These unhealthy institutional or structural barriers can lead to misogyny, racism, and homophobia. Rather than seeking the involvement and leadership of the community, the institution creates a barrier between itself and its own constituents, implying that the institution knows what is in the best interests of the people, even more than the people do. This barrier impedes the development of sustainable leadership from within the community. It also negates the possibility of shared responsibility, hope, and resilience for the future.

An example of an indigenous barrier might be when a minority or marginalized population creates a specialized group to preserve its identity within a larger structure that is designed to serve or benefit a different population—for example, a Latino student organization on a predominantly white college campus. Such groups are not examples of reverse racism or unhealthy barriers; rather, they are constructed to preserve culture and ethnic identity amid structural barriers that threaten their humanity and well-being.

Indigenous barriers and spaces are especially needed in countries that have a history of colonialism or have ongoing discrimination and disparity toward Indigenous or minority populations. Canada's Truth and Reconciliation Commission is a great example of a national effort to correct institutional wrongs done to Indigenous communities. Testimony of thousands of residential school survivors who endured sexual abuse and cultural genocide was heard, and this led to ninety-four recommendations to repair relationship between Aboriginal peoples and the rest of Canada.[3] Faith leaders have also been urging the prime minister to pass a bill to enshrine the United Nations Declaration on the Rights of Indigenous Peoples (UNDRIP) into Canadian law and, in consultation with Indigenous peoples, implement a national plan to achieve the UN objectives.[4]

When barriers become institutionalized, systemic injustice and violence can result, even when they were intended for good. The prison system, which we referenced as an example of an external barrier, was started by Quakers as a means of rehabilitation. The penitentiary, originally designed to encourage penitence through silence and reflection, has become a behemoth. The size and impact of the prison system in the United States has quadrupled over the last forty years, even as rates of crime have remained relatively stable. Incarceration has become a multibillion-dollar industry, with private prisons profiting from the misery and misfortune of mostly poor, minority, and mentally ill citizens.[5] Over half of those in prison are in for nonviolent offenses, which still carry excessively long sentences; those who complete their sentences leave with a permanent record that bars them from reintegration into society as full citizens.[6] Rates of incarceration among women and youth are on the rise as well.[7]

---

3. "Truth and Reconciliation Commission Urges Canada to Confront 'Cultural Genocide' of Residential Schools," CBC News, last updated June 3, 2015, http://www.cbc .ca/news/politics/truth-and-reconciliation-commission-urges-canada-to-confront-cultural-genocide-of-residential-schools-1.3096229.

4. Joelle Kidd, "Hiltz Urges Prime Minister to Support Bill C-262," *Anglican Journal*, November 16, 2017, http://www.anglicanjournal.com/articles/hiltz-urges-prime-minister-support-bill-c-262/.

5. For a concise synopsis of who profits from the prison industrial complex, see Angela Davis, "The Prison Industrial Complex," chap. 5 in *Are Prisons Obsolete?* (New York: Seven Stories Press, 2003).

6. Prison Policy Initiative, "Mass Incarceration: The Whole Pie 2017," March 14, 2017, https://www.prisonpolicy.org/reports/pie2017.html.

7. The Sentencing Project, "Trends in U.S. Corrections: Fact Sheet," June 2017, http:// www.sentencingproject.org/publications/trends-in-u-s-corrections/.

Without deep examination of institutional systems and without intentional corrections in policy, societal injustice can become a permanent fixture of our social landscape. Without accountability, all institutions are capable of causing harm and injustice. This is why the pivot from barriers to bridge building is crucial if we are to see a more just world for everyone.

LIVE IN TENSION, LIVE INTENTION: THE PIVOT TO BRIDGE BUILDING

Bridges connect two opposite and nonadjacent sides. A bridge builder finds common ground and creates access between opposing sides and groups. "Bridgers" seek to understand and sit in the tension, just like an actual tension bridge. While bridgers extend relationship to both sides, this does not mean they remain neutral in the face of injustice. Because they are open to mediating conflict, they know when to lean, when to challenge, and when to dismantle barriers to true reconciliation.

A person or community committed to bridge building has two essential characteristics: living intention and living in tension. What we mean by *living intention* is that people who are committed to bridge building take purposeful, thoughtful actions in how they "do life" and how they engage others. Bridgers do the sometimes arduous work of anticipating how what they say or how they say it will affect other people and how it will affect community transformation. Essentially, bridgers live their lives on purpose, by design.

So often, especially in this age of technology and social media, no sooner do we have a thought in our heads than we have shared it—quite literally—with the world! Less and less do we take the time to think about the impact our statement will have on recipients or the initiatives we are so passionate about, let alone whether the mode of communication we choose is the most appropriate or effective. We run with the idea that everything is "textable" or "tweetable": that everything can be conveyed in the allotted amount of characters. We often claim that our objective in communicating a challenging or prophetic message in this manner is for others to consider a fresh perspective. We say that it is our contribution to "changing the world." But sometimes the true goal appears to be simply getting it off our chests, which is a much more self-serving motive than actually creating space for others to consider a fresh perspective.

Bridgers often apply a methodology to considering how and when they communicate. They consider their objective *before* selecting what they will say and when and how they will say it. This is one example of how we can all live more intentionally. Other examples include when, how, and where we spend our money; who benefits from what we consume; how much space we take up in the world; what size footprint we are leaving; the implications of that footprint for people who experience less privilege than we do; and finally, with whom we share our lives and relationships. Purposeful decision-making around these topics heightens the chance that we will make a more positive impact on ourselves, our community, and the world.

The other essential characteristic of effective bridge building is *living in tension*. How have we been acculturated to respond to relationship challenges? What do we do when we don't share opinions or beliefs with those in our community of faith or our family? The pervading messages around us give us full permission to separate, part ways, and sever ties. We do not have a lot of practice in how to do life together when we don't see things eye to eye. Bridgers recognize the value of working *through* difficult issues, and they become skilled at facilitating this process with the people around them. Bridgers develop a commitment to living *in* the tension, recognizing that sometimes such tension is a condition to be managed rather than a problem to be solved. They come to accept the uncertainty, showing up to the possibility and even creating the invitation to resolution and reconciliation. But bridgers also at times relinquish power over a situation, knowing that trying to wrest control of a solution can entice groups to fabricate "pseudo-resolutions" that aren't sustainable.

Both *living intention* and *living in tension* require sacrifice. It takes time to think through life decisions and to live our lives purposefully. There is a discernment process inherent in living intentionally and in living in tension, so these can be slower and sometimes more arduous ways of living. For example, living intentionally might mean shopping locally. This often requires us to physically go to a store or to wait longer for our deliveries than we would if we pursued more expeditious online shopping experiences. Walking and using public transportation often call for more planning and more time. Similarly, living in tension means being present to angst and discomfort; it means sometimes enduring strained relationships. It means not knowing *when* an issue or challenge will be resolved, if ever. And in both cases—living intention and living in tension—the bridger is vulnerable, exposed to the discomfort of inconvenience and unknowing. And bridgers know that others witness them in this exposed place of being a living sacrifice. But get this: it is through our own willingness to expose ourselves as vulnerable and uncertain that others become liberated to become bridge builders as well!

Several years ago, I (Reesheda) served as a school administrator. I started as a school principal and gradually moved up the ranks, ultimately serving as the leader of nine school principals and their schools. My identity was pretty wrapped up in my role as a successful school leader. To be honest, I am not sure I made much effort to find my identity in much else at that time. My tenure in that role ended in termination, which was the result of systemic injustice. To say that I was devastated is an absolute understatement. I remember feeling despondent for days after receiving the news, and I can still summon the feeling of confusion I experienced, wondering, If I am not this, then what am I?

Compound the shock of identity loss with the shame of termination, and the result was an incredibly awkward, fumbled response to friends and colleagues, who all inevitably asked, "So what are you up to now? And what happened with your school leadership role?" Suffice it to say, it was not my go-to response to say, "Well, I was terminated from my position, and now, as a result, I have no idea who I am." Eight years after the fact, however, I now know that *every* prophetic justice leader whose work I appreciate has experienced some form of marginalization, termination, or isolation, usually as a direct result of the work itself.

As this reality has become clearer to me, I have become committed to vulnerability and transparency about my own narrative so that others might be liberated from the shame and embarrassment of malignment. This sacrifice is an inherent part of the work, and my ability to share it as such is a tool of liberation for others to emerge from self-blame.

So now, when I talk about that season of my life, I am *intentional* about shamelessly naming that I was terminated as a result of systemic injustice. The irony: the more I tell the story, the more I hear others' stories of termination because of systemic injustice and imbalanced power structures. I receive the gift of community. Together, we can live purposefully into the tension of such injustices.

THREE SHIFTS TOWARD BRIDGE BUILDING

The pivot from barriers to bridge building is characterized by three important shifts toward conversation, compassion, and community.

Conversation: Dialogue versus debate

Learning to dialogue is a crucial skill for any bridge builder. Debates are designed to create clear winners and losers. Nobody enjoys being a loser, so debates often get heated and can escalate to name-calling or, in some cases, even physical fights. Debates often devolve into pounding one's opponents into the ground, showing how wrong, stupid, and silly they are to believe what they believe. Debate has become the dominant method of political, religious, and academic discourse. After all, most schools have debate teams, not dialogue teams.

2.2 Three shifts

	Barriers	to	Bridge building
Shift 1: Conversation	Debate	→	Dialogue
Shift 2: Compassion	Walls	→	Welcome
Shift 3: Community	Competition	→	Collaboration

But dialogue is a method that opens lines of communication. Dialogue involves listening to learn, as well as speaking to inform. Dialogue allows for mutual learning. In a debate, no one is willing to learn, because no one wants to give any ground to the other side. In dialogue, someone can admit that she or he is in process and has much to learn. In dialogue, it is possible to affirm what we have in common and to clarify where tension exists. Dialogue is more conducive for relationships than debate.

Dialogue requires humility and an acknowledgment that no one's thinking is infallible. As the apostle Paul said, "For now we see in a mirror, dimly" (1 Corinthians 13:12). No one has all the answers. No one sees everything in its entirety. Everyone's perspective is limited and vulnerable to bias. Dialogue recognizes that people of different parties, religions, and cultures may have important perspectives and insights to offer. Dialogue is an art that provides a way of communicating with both friends and foes. My (Shawn's) father-in-law is a fundamentalist Christian, and my sister-in-law is an agnostic. We have had some pretty intense conversations over the years. But because we are able to dialogue together, we are able to see different truths we may not have seen before.

Debate is about strategy and competition, which often leads to secrecy, as no one wants the opponent to know one's plan or expectations. But dialogue should have clear and established "rules of engagement" that all parties create, agree to, and own. It is important to establish this tone from the beginning so that all participants know what to expect and can anticipate how to handle themselves as a part of the dialogue.

Recently, I (Reesheda) helped to facilitate a panel discussion about the movie *Get Out*. Often referred to as a social thriller, *Get Out* is a provocative movie that challenges its viewers to think about how Black bodies and the Black experience are exploited, co-opted, and objectified. People from all walks of life received a public invitation to come to L!VE Café to listen to two panels, both quite diverse in their composition, and to grapple with questions related to the controversial film. As the facilitator who curated both panels, I was very careful about the messaging the audience received before the panelists' participation.

I told the seventy people in the room that we were *not* attempting to create safe space. We were trying to create a space for learning—with all the dignity, grace, and love we could muster in the midst of what would inevitably make us uncomfortable. I gave everyone the opportunity to quietly consider what that would mean for them as listeners and as participants. After a minute or two, I reminded everyone of the objectives of the dialogue: to grapple with ideas around race and to wrestle with different ideas. Doing so would be messy, I said, and it might cause us to shift back and forth between ideological positions and perhaps not settle into any one perspective.

What resulted was a dynamic exchange of ideas, questions, and ponderings. A mutual vulnerability filled the room in a way that dialogue offers and debate never does. Because panelists and audience members alike were willing to embody vulnerability, we were challenged by each other's candor and learned a great deal about each person's perspective. This made room to reconsider what we thought we knew coming into the experience.

At the end of the evening, I challenged each person in the room to find someone she or he did not know and who did not look or sound like her or him. I encouraged the pairs to then dialogue about this experience. As I walked around the room and listened in on some of the conversations, I heard people say how important it was for them to have heard, *before* we started, that they would be uncomfortable and challenged. Those words gave them the space to prepare so that when those moments of discomfort came, they were ready for it.

Setting the tone and creating a culture in which dialogue prevails over debate increases the frequency of risk-taking and courageous conversations.

Compassion: Welcome versus walls

Soul force is motivated by deep compassion, love, and empathy. A pivot to compassion allows us to see, hear, and welcome people who are different from ourselves.

Miea Walker, a friend of ours who works in prison reform, spent nine years in a women's prison, where she underwent a significant spiritual transformation. After she was released and could physically leave the prison, she still wrestled with internal barriers of shame and judgment. Even when she spoke at churches, she felt that people saw her past rather than who she had become. Her question to Christians now is: "Do you see me? Do you see me in my humanity? Do you see me as a sister?" She urges us to no longer call people who are in prison or who were once in prison *inmates*, *convicts*, or *felons*. Instead, she calls us to see them as brothers and sisters. Instead of building up walls, whether internal or external, Walker challenges us to offer compassion and welcome.

Hospitality is a tangible way to practice compassion. I (Shawn) have learned about hospitality from my neighbors in the city. I remember bringing a new group of Mission Year volunteers into Little Village, a predominantly Mexican immigrant neighborhood on the West Side of Chicago. The volunteers were coming from rural and suburban areas to spend a year building authentic relationships, loving their neighbors, and learning to live out compassion and justice. As soon as I pulled the van up to the curb, we were met by a host of people eager to welcome their new neighbors. The neighbors showed up to help the volunteers bring their bags up three flights of stairs to the apartment where they would be living. This wasn't a coordinated event. My goal actually had been to move the volunteers in as inconspicuously as possible. But their Little Village neighbors were showing them a spontaneous and heartfelt example of what compassion and hospitality looks like across dividing lines of class and culture.

Afterward, I wanted to make sure that the team of volunteers understood the significance of what had happened. I asked them to imagine if the roles were reversed. If their new Mexican neighbors had moved into their hometowns, would they have received the same welcome? The answer was a unanimous no. The very first interaction these Mission Year volunteers had in the city offered them a lesson in hospitality. It provided a challenge to extend this same hospitality and compassion that they had received.

In our polarized political climate, it's easy to demonize those who think, vote, or believe differently. Both of us are often asked to speak in a variety of contexts along the conservative-liberal spectrum. One week I (Shawn) was asked to speak at a very conservative church about God's heart for the poor. I knew that what I was going to share would be challenging for some people in the audience.

I used the text of Matthew 25 and spoke about God's concern for the poor, the immigrant, and the prisoner, three groups of people who are especially vulnerable to structural barriers. By the end of the talk, the room was dead silent, and I had no read on what the people in the crowd were thinking. The pastor told the congregation I would be at a table in the back if anyone wanted to buy a book or talk to me. I expected to be left standing by myself awkwardly.

Surprisingly, many people came up to talk. One man, who identified himself as ultraconservative, said that while we may not see eye to eye on every political issue, he resonated with the compassionate approach to people I presented. I found myself connecting unexpectedly with several other church members around a shared empathy toward people on the margins who were experiencing pain. During that trip, I realized that compassion is a bridge. It may, in fact, be one of the most powerful bridges. So much of our political discourse and policy lacks compassion. What if we started there? What if we started by seeing people as people rather than issues? What if we listened to each other's stories before listing our talking points?

Compassion is an invitation to reimagine and reshape our world. The segregation, division, and hostility that is so prevalent is not inevitable. We have the power to write a new story. It is possible to live differently, to diversify our social networks, and to reimagine the institutional structures of our world. It is not only possible; it is essential.

Community: Collaboration versus competition
So much of our society is designed around competition, from the sports teams we follow to the churches we attend.

Many of our neighborhoods have dozens of churches, yet how often do they come together? There's a large church in Texas that houses over thirteen diverse congregations inside its massive walls throughout the week. The thirteen congregations reflect a range of ethnic cultures and denominational affiliations. Yet one staff member lamented to us that the thirteen distinct groups rarely, if ever, interact with one another. If churches cannot collaborate even when they are in the same building, how are we going to come together in our cities and across regions? Our competition is limiting our collective potential and robbing our communities of greater spiritual and social impact.

As the executive director of a national nonprofit, I (Reesheda) often see this dynamic play itself out as it pertains to fundraising and development. Frequently, five hundred to a thousand organizations apply for the same $50,000 grant. The odds of any one organization receiving the grant are extremely small. But the worst effect of this situation is the competitive landscape created by institutions who often share missional alignment. Rather than collaborating toward a common mission, the organizations become reluctant to share their "secret sauce," for fear that their counterparts might leverage this knowledge to get the grant. The supreme irony is that this very kind of competition produces a countermissional effect for all the competing organizations, leaving them further and further behind in realizing their mission. Organizations often wind up closing their doors because of a lack of funding. If they could work together and collaborate, however, the resources they need to realize the mission would likely become available.

Competition can thwart bridge building. When life is defined in terms of winning and losing, compassion is often squeezed out. This is why sports fans often cheer when an opponent's player is injured: their tribal identity supersedes a universal concern for humanity. A competitive mindset can create barriers to community. When a nation values competition over collaboration and cooperation, division is often bred. When the economy of a nation is based on competition, there are inevitable winners and losers. As long as we are winning, it's great. But once we start falling behind or getting into an economic hole, we realize it's not fun anymore. Anyone who has played Monopoly knows it's a great feeling when you're winning, but when you're losing, all you want to do is flip the game board over and walk away!

When we direct our soul force into collaborative partnerships instead of competitive ones, we increase our mental peace, relationships, and even our bottom line.[8] It can be a hard shift, but it opens up so much possibility. When we see others as potential collaborators, we widen our circle of friends and enhance our individual and collective well-being. The next pivot will build on this collaborative spirit as it relates to moving toward local and global solidarity.

SOUL FORCE STORY

From barriers to bridge building

Timothy Hoekstra

In 1991 a team of us started a new church that would be built on the church growth principle of homogeneity: simply reach out to people who are like you, and your church will come together and grow. In our case, that would be white, middle- to upper-middle-class suburbanites. And for the first few years, that principle seemed to work. We soon became a church of three to four hundred people, with no end of growth in sight.

But then, through a series of challenges, things began to change. One of those changes was the growing vision of a group of men in our church who began to desire the experience of more of the diversity of God's kingdom. We began to pray for it, and to seek it in our hearts. We were unsure of where to begin, but we knew that God would be the one to show us the way.

---

8. For anecdotal evidence and research on how cooperative activities beat competition, check out Alfie Kohn, *No Contest: The Case against Competition* (New York: Houghton Mifflin, 1992).

In 1998 our church and its story took a significant shift, and everything changed. Through a series of relationships, we were introduced to a sixty-seven-year-old pastor from the West Side of Chicago named Rev. Clarence Hilliard. He was the founding and current pastor of Austin Corinthian Baptist Church at that time. He had worked with Martin Luther King and had debated Malcolm X, and he had a rich knowledge and understanding of Black history and biblical perspectives.

When I first met Rev. Hilliard in January 1998, he immediately challenged me. I had indicated an interest in learning more about diversity in the church. His response was epic. "Tim, I have no time for a once-a-year Black History Month experience. But if you want to move forward together in a real relationship, then be ready for the deal to come down on you for hanging around Black folks."

Interestingly, my heart was being stirred by the Holy Spirit, and that stirring produced my response. "I am willing to take that challenge on, and I don't have any desire to bring anything to you or your church from us," I said. "We simply want to submit ourselves to you and your church to listen and be taught."

Everything began to change! Many of us from our suburban, white church began to gather with some of their members at their weekly Wednesday morning praise, prayer, and Bible study time at six o'clock. This then would be followed by breakfast at Marvin's Soul Food Restaurant across the street. I often had to depart my house before five o'clock to attend these gatherings. But it was at the breakfast table that I listened, asked questions, and learned. After a few months, we invited this influential pastor to preach a message at our church. Soon after that message, the first exit of fifteen households from our church took place. The deal started to come down. Still, we believed God had called for and was leading this relationship.

We slowly built in more times of gathering, continuing with Wednesday mornings, gathering with our men and eventually men and women on every first Saturday, and finally even working in a monthly worship time together at their church every second

Sunday of the month. On that Sunday, in order to prioritize our evening gathering at their church, we didn't gather in the morning but only at five in the evening out in Austin for dinner and worship together.

Now, nearly twenty years later, all these gatherings continue. And most of those gatherings include many members of other churches. Our fellowship now consists of four churches: one from the North Side of the city, one from the South Side of the city, Austin Corinthian from the West Side, and our church from the west suburbs.

We continued to learn from Rev. Hilliard for seven years before the Lord took him home after a battle with cancer. At that point, many in both churches thought the relationship might end. But it did not. We have continued to move forward together, with no sense that this relationship will ever end. Our congregation is committed to the healing of the racial divide as we work toward justice. This is our top priority. It influences our financial decisions and has led us to make a decision to never own a building or property out in the suburbs. As we submit to the Black leaders and churches of Chicago's West Side, we seek to carry the call for racial healing and justice wherever we go in the suburbs and city.

The original name that I gave our church back in 1991 was Suburban Life Community Church. You can see where our vision was. But today that name is reinterpreted: Sub-Urban Life Community Church. We are a church that is informed in its life by living under the Black leaders and churches of Chicago. Everything has changed . . . and is changing!

SOUL FORCE PIVOT POINTS

Live in tension

Commit to sit in the tension before the conversation begins. Recognize that different perspectives will be shared and that the ultimate goal is not to agree or convince the other but to hear each other and seek understanding. Stay at the table even if or when it gets heated. Remember: Jesus called his disciples to love one another, not agree with one another.

Live intention

Be thoughtful about how you are existing in yourself, in your relationships, and in your community. Reflect on how you are showing up. Consider what and how you consume and what and how you steward. Assess what you are keeping or holding and what you are dispensing with or giving away.

Ask why

Too often we ask what someone believes without asking why. Hearing what someone believes is only part of the story. Many of our assumptions about people we disagree with are actually false, because we have jumped to conclusions. So often we build up arguments in our head before we have fully understood where another person is coming from. Seek to understand first. Be curious. Ask questions.

Share stories

When we are talking with people who have strong negative stereotypes about the city or people we live and work with, we share stories that provide a counternarrative. The story may not change their mind, but it at least provides a counterbalance to a one-sided or false narrative. People may or may not be moved by statistics, but they are almost always moved by story.

Stay open

Be willing to learn from those you disagree with, and be open to changing your mind. In order for dialogue to be authentic, both parties need to be willing to change in light of new information or perspectives. Ashleigh Hill, a friend of ours, is always advising young people, "It's okay to change your mind." Most of us don't think the same way we did ten or fifteen years ago. Hopefully all of us are continuing to adapt our views as we learn and encounter new people, places, and ideas.

Be humble

Remember, we only see in part, so don't be a jerk. (That's a paraphrase of the apostle Paul.) Being right is not the end goal. We can be right but still lack love. Being loving is more important than being right. Having character and humility in how we talk gives greater credence to what we are saying. No matter how much education or experience we have, our viewpoints are limited.

Find common ground

Bridge builders look for common ground. We may not be on the same side of every issue, but we can find commonalities with others. Establishing common ground safeguards against demonizing people who disagree and allows us to engage others with dignity.

Examine institutional systems

Without accountability, all systems are capable of causing harm and injustice. We cannot assume that simply because a system is working for us, or some people, it is working for all people. Listen to the voices of people who are experiencing the detrimental effects of certain systems. This listening can help us look critically at institutional structures and begin to imagine a more just and hopeful world.

PIVOT 2 MANTRA

I will build bridges.

Pivot 3

FROM SELF-CENTEREDNESS TO SOLIDARITY

Solidarity does not assume that our struggles are the same struggles, or that our pain is the same pain, or that our hope is for the same future. Solidarity involves commitment, and work, as well as the recognition that even if we do not have the same feelings, or the same lives, or the same bodies, we do live on common ground.
—SARA AHMED, *THE CULTURAL POLITICS OF EMOTION*

Recently, I (Reesheda) had the pleasure of attending a performance of *Hamilton* in Chicago. *Hamilton* is a musical about the life of one of America's founding fathers, Alexander Hamilton. Written and scored by Lin-Manuel Miranda, the performance embodies the essential elements of hip-hop culture: emceeing, deejaying, break dancing, and graffitiing. As I walked into the theater lobby, I was immediately struck by the sheer number of white or otherwise dominant-culture people who were there to see the show.

I smiled to myself, thinking about the crowd who had caused the show to sell out at over $200 a ticket. Do all these people know that the cast of *Hamilton* is predominantly composed of people of

color? I wondered. And do they know that the performance is
infused with all four elements of hip-hop culture?

Now, of course, no one buys a $200 theater ticket without
knowing about the composition of the performance. So really, the
bigger question was, *Why* are all these people from the dominant
culture willing to pay exorbitantly to witness this inclusive retell-
ing of history?

A big question, I know. But there's an irony here. The history
that unfolded in the United States—a history of enslavement and
oppression—has offered white and dominant-culture people privilege and entitlement. That same privilege now allows them the
security and wealth to pay top dollar to witness this musical's
countercultural depiction of history and culture—a depiction that
calls into question everything about the self-preserving and exclu-
sive lifestyle many of them are living.

The fact that so many white and dominant-culture participants
paid sizable sums to see *Hamilton* says that they like to imagine
an American history that is inclusive, polylithic, multicultural, and
rich with countercultural narratives. They like the *idea* of such a
past and present.

The challenge, however, is to move beyond *imagining* to *enacting* actual solidarity. Solidarity is the movement from *I* to *we*. It
doesn't mean we neglect ourselves, but it means we see that our
well-being is tied to the well-being of others. Solidarity means
acknowledging that we have responsibility beyond taking care of
ourselves; we have a responsibility to make sure that our neighbors,
next door and globally, are taken care of as well. In its essence,
solidarity is love and universal concern for humanity. Solidarity
happens when we make other people's problems our problems.

To do this, we have to be willing to pivot from self-centeredness
to solidarity.

WHY ARE WE SELF-CENTERED?

Sadly, most of what we do that does not serve us or others well
is born out of fear. Self-centeredness is the life, love, and legacy
snatcher in our families, in our country, and in our world.

In 1933 Franklin Delano Roosevelt said in his first inaugural address, "The only thing we have to fear is fear itself." That was more than eighty years ago, and in the ensuing years, we have become even more skilled in fear's applications. Self-preservation is born out of fear. We now skillfully serve and preserve ourselves, personally and in the ways we lead. Even as collectives—whether social or organizational or political bodies—we often operate out of self-preservation. We are afraid of what we will lose for ourselves, in our leadership, and in our social circles. We thus abandon the possibility of living a life rich with discoveries that are uncovered only through lives lived in solidarity with one another.

We exchange a truly rich life for one that demands every moment of our attention to keep watch over the "stuff" it has produced. Yet if we told the whole truth, the quality of this life is not as fulfilling as a life lived in solidarity with others.

It is important to note the distinction between self-centeredness and self-care. Self-centeredness can be a hindrance to movement, because it prevents true solidarity with others. Self-care is a necessity for movement, because it restores and sustains us on the journey toward solidarity.

PERSONAL SELF-CENTEREDNESS

Personal self-centeredness is definitely the most counterproductive form of self-centeredness. Honestly, we all want to be in loving relationships with other people—relationships in which we feel valued and respected and in which we offer love, value, and respect in return. Yet inevitably we allow fear to overcome us. When we do, we begin to ask ourselves what people are trying to take from us, how that will affect our ability to preserve what we have, and how their efforts will keep us from moving forward and acquiring more stuff.

It is not difficult to make the connection between how these thoughts might easily thrust us into behaviors that deteriorate loving relationships or even the potential for them. And there, friends, is the irony. We perpetually trade in the thing we want the most—true, long-lasting relationships—for the thing that dominant culture *tells us* we should value: stuff. We acquire more and more stuff, thinking that maybe we just haven't gotten enough of it to reach our full, blissful capacity. But as we acquire more and more—whether education, salary, real estate, titles and positions, or power and authority—we use every ounce of energy we have to preserve it all. We leave no time for being fully present to ourselves or the relationships we say matter so much to us. Something within us starts to whisper in discontent. As we get older, the voice becomes louder: "This. Ain't. It."

We may ignore this voice at first, which is easy to do when it is drowned out by all the demands of preserving all that we have. But over time, it nags us, compels us to examine it further.

This energy that thrusts us into questioning more deeply the purpose of our lives? That is soul force! The drive that pushes us to reexamine dormant passions for our communities? That is soul force! Rather than allowing culture to dictate to us that we must live lives of isolation, obsession, and individualism, we

3.1 Three forms of personal self-centeredness

Self-centeredness	Lie	Behavior	Pivot to solidarity
Loss and pain avoidance	"I will be more comfortable and avoid pain if I just take care of myself."	Justify the need to be self-centered for the sake of self-protection and avoiding loss	Accept healthy discomfort in order to have deeper relationships and a life filled with greater value and purpose
Preservation	"If I take care of myself and my things, I get to keep what I have."	Ignore the needs of others in order to keep what you have intact	Embrace the idea that some of what we have acquired is for the purpose of sharing with those who would benefit from receiving it
Consumption	"If I just had more stuff, I would be safer, more cared for, and happier."	Act as though material wealth is something you deserve	Shift from acquiring more to examining how to best leverage what you already have on behalf of others

have the power—the soul force—to create new culture that frees us to live our lives in solidarity. We begin to ask ourselves what is most valuable: preserving a prescribed culture of self-centeredness that does not lead to fulfillment, or designing a life of deep, mutual relationships.

Andy Crouch, in his book *Culture Making: Recovering Our Creative Calling*, says that if we wish to live in ways contrary to what currently exists, then we will have to create it. He asserts that any culture we create will need to "persuade our neighbors to set aside some existing set of cultural goods for our new proposal."[1] We will need to move beyond condemning culture, critiquing culture, copying culture, and consuming culture to what Crouch refers to as "the art of cultivation."[2] Notice that individuals cannot create culture by themselves. Rather, it will take the lot of us, moving from self-centeredness to solidarity together, to create a movement toward courageous and abundant living!

One obstacle to considering how culture is created is the way in which we have been divided up, sectioned off, and categorized, resulting in separation and division rather than cohesion and solidarity. We have divisions of religion, race, gender, class—you name it, we can divide it!

Even as we were writing this book, race-based division was causing violence and death on the streets of Charlottesville, Virginia. Rooted in capitalism, consumption, and power preservation, race as a social construct has pervaded our country and our world. And while it has certainly made life materially comfortable for the majority culture, it has been at the expense of our true collective identity. We will never know who we would be as individuals or as a country without the blight of racism.

These social constructs have been erected to ensure that certain creeds, doctrines, and ideologies flourish. And while particular beliefs have been maintained through these divisive systems, we, the people, are not flourishing, nor are the systems in which we live.

---

1. Andy Crouch, *Culture Making: Recovering Our Creative Calling* (Downers Grove, IL: InterVarsity Press, 2008), 67.

2. Ibid., 73.

LEADERSHIP SELF-CENTEREDNESS

It is a fallacy that when we go to work, we leave our "personal selves" at home. We take our whole selves with us everywhere we go. Individuals who practice personal self-centeredness and take on a leadership role often become self-centered leaders. Fear is at the center of carrying out this model of leadership as well. When we as leaders see ourselves at the center of our organizations, the people and the mission become peripheral. This self-centeredness leaves us susceptible to being blindsided by our own narcissism, insulation, and grandiosity.

I (Reesheda) once led an elementary school located in the Englewood neighborhood in Chicago. It was my first year as a school principal, so to say that I was still getting my sea legs about me as an administrator would be an understatement! I knew that there were things I still needed to learn, and I didn't even always know what those things were. I was one of the youngest principals in the

3.2 Three forms of leadership self-centeredness

Self-centeredness	Lie	Behavior	Pivot to solidarity
Narcissism	"I am the leader because I am the only one who knows what I know and can do what I can do."	Take credit and reward for all that goes well	Share successes with all who helped to attain them
Defensiveness	"If I don't make myself the center of it all, I will not be respected or perceived as a strong leader, and I will lose my ability to lead."	Overcompensate and take a blaming and defensive stance when things do not go well	See challenges and failures as opportunities for collective learning and growth; own these moments together with the solidarity group
Authoritarianism	"Leadership is always rooted in hierarchical power."	Micromanage teams; squelch the gifts and talents of others; abuse power for selfish ambition	Share access to power, wealth, and decision-making with those working to build the mission; empower others to live courageously

district, and certainly one of the greenest, and I was also working in a school that had not received the level of empowerment and support that the amazing students and staff there deserved. There were lagging and antiquated systems in place, and there was much work to do to implement a quality education plan for our students. Knowing that so much needed to be done—and knowing how inexperienced I was—made for a wicked combination in the heart and mind of this new school principal!

I had a ton of networks I could plug into: one that supported school leaders whose schools need better math and science curriculum; one that supported school leaders who had a significant number of special education students; even one that met at the local pub on Friday evenings to drown their sorrows in w(h)ine! But none of these networks were composed of people who really knew me. None were made up of people I trusted and could trust, people with whom I could be vulnerable and with whom I could share my fears and inadequacies as a leader.

So, like everyone else in those cohorts, I showed up at those events and presented my best, most confident self! I shined a positive light on my school, overcompensating for all the ill-perceived notions that people have about a little elementary school in Englewood. I and the others in these groups hid behind our professionalism, maintaining the status quo and solidifying our personal successes. As a result, none of those folks could assist me in being a transformational leader who stood in solidarity with my school.

Contrast this with a network that was then called New Leaders for New Schools, which I and one hundred other principals-in-training throughout the country experienced the previous year. There I acquired four solid relationships with members of my cohort who lived in Chicago and who were having a very similar experience in their own first year as principals. Having journeyed together the entire year before we began leading our own schools, we had cultivated true, deep, authentic relationships. These would be our saving grace in the year and years to come.

With these four women I would initially present my Teflon-tough leadership armor—until they said things that disarmed me and made me tell my truth. Their questions and comments unearthed my fears and trepidation in a way that allowed them to see what I really needed and sometimes even offer effective solutions. With these four women I conversed about work, life, kids, relationships, and self, all interwoven, so that I could examine holistic solutions for how to live and lead. Through mutual solidarity, we gradually saw our true leadership capacity surface, and we began to claim it more resolutely, honoring people over systems, others over self, and change over monikers.

And get this: it was that informal gathering of five struggling principals—not the formal networks with which we were connected—that made us grow and evolve as leaders. In fact, when we got smart about how we tapped into our true relationships, we became better at utilizing and mobilizing of all our resources, including our networks, on behalf of the community.

Interestingly enough, none of us are principals today; however, all of us continue to be leaders, and the organizations we have chosen to lead are centered in "otherness": social enterprise, mentoring and coaching programs, and history and legacy preservation. When the five of us finally figured out that leadership is not about the preservation of ourselves, our "stuff," or our titles, but about letting go, empowering, and being vulnerable, we could share access to what we had learned with so many others.

SOCIETAL AND INSTITUTIONAL SELF-CENTEREDNESS

Developing and establishing institutions takes a great deal of work. A significant number of people are involved in the creation and maintenance of them, and those charged with the preservation of institutions do their absolute best to ensure the longevity of what so many have sacrificed to build. Yet an interesting phenomenon frequently unfolds: when people are too driven by the desire to preserve an institution, they sometimes neglect to consider the effect that maintaining the institution is having on the people associated with it. Institutional leaders can become so busy preserving

3.3 Three forms of societal and institutional self-centeredness

Self-centeredness	Lie	Behavior	Pivot to solidarity
Institutionalism	"If we take care of the organization, it will take care of us."	Prioritize the organization over the people it serves	Focus on the people affected by the organization, prioritizing their care over the institution itself
Perpetuity	"Our main mission is to preserve the organization so it will last forever."	Focus more on the longevity of the organization than on whether the mission is being accomplished	Be open to endings and the lament and dignity inherent in them as a way of life rather than a disaster
Expansion	"Getting bigger and expanding our territory is a sign of God's blessing and organizational effectiveness."	Focus more on size and growth than on whether expansion is worthwhile, necessary, or relevant	Measure achievement according to positive, collective impact rather than number of participants

and expanding the institutions themselves that they neglect the very *people* the institutions were designed to support.

Instead of caring for the ones who are doing the work and sustaining the institution, the workers are seen as disposable and are sacrificed for the sake of the organization. This can create a toxic culture in which employees dread going to work even though they may believe strongly in the mission of the institution. This is not limited to large corporations either. We have seen churches, Christian mission organizations, and community nonprofits fall into this pattern as well. Rather than believe the lie that taking care of the organization will be best for the workers, we have found the exact opposite to be true. When we take care of staff, create a healthy work culture, and demonstrate concern for staff members as whole people, we find they become even more committed to the organization's mission.

One slogan that has become quite popular among nonprofits is "Poverty is expensive." This statement is intended to underscore the idea that those who have the least (materially speaking) are usually expected to pay the most for goods and services. But the phrase has been subverted as a means by which institutions underscore their need for more support from their donor base. The party line goes as follows: poverty costs a lot of money; if you want to avoid the perils that will come if poor people are not taken care of, then you should donate more money to us so that we can manage the problem of poverty. (And yes, many nonprofit institutions see themselves as "taking care" of those in poverty.)

By playing on the perception that the poor need institutions to take care of their problems, institutions have managed to perpetuate, sustain, and even expand themselves—even while very little data substantiates the idea that their work truly addresses the challenges of poverty.

As ten thousand baby boomers retire each day, the notion of "legacy projects" has gained currency. Legacy projects are intended to make the past and present work of the leader indelible and long lasting. Some examples of legacy projects including providing water to an entire country or ensuring the welfare of single mothers. Legacy is certainly on the hearts and minds of leaders transitioning into retirement.[3] These leaders, many of whom have founded the organizations they lead, are asking themselves, "What can I do at the end of my tenure that will make the most impact on how people remember me as a leader?"

Undoubtedly, this is a natural question to consider when one has invested so much into a cause and an organization. We are, after all, meaning-making machines, and we want to ensure that we have passed on the meaning of our work to those around us, even as we transition into a new season of life.

It is important, however, to hold more than one imperative at a time. As emerging retirees consider how to solidify their vocational legacy, they must also consider, with just as much conviction, what is best for the community or organization they serve. They must

3. D'vera Cohn and Paul Taylor, "Baby Boomers Approach 65—Glumly," Pew Research Center, December 20, 2010, http://www.pewsocialtrends.org/2010/12/20/baby-boomers-approach-65-glumly/.

consider not only their own legacies but the lives of those affected by the decisions they make.

If you are a leader who is soon to retire, we as Gen Xers implore you: Even as you consider your own legacy, consider a "placemaking" plan for the next generation of leaders. Many organizations suffer from "founder's sydrome," where the founder of an organization maintains a firm hold of power and shows no intention or plan to transition out. Instead, consider developing a transition plan, including a peaceable and effective handover of power. Help young leaders transition into viable roles and mentor them throughout the time of transition. Organizational endurance and sustainability are essential parts of a rich legacy.

In many instances, people undergird institutions through charitable gift annuities, trusts, and bequests. Often, in our quest to feel as though we have contributed, we neglect to examine if we've actually created sustainable change or only contributed funds that help us feel better about how we are showing up in the world. Going beyond the financial contribution and taking a deeper dive into the true impact that institutions are having on the lives of the people: this is one very significant way by which we can move from self-centeredness to solidarity.

FROM *I* TO *WE*: THE PIVOT TOWARD SOLIDARITY

Growing up in white Christian culture, I (Shawn) was instilled with a moral conscience. Faith, politics, and financial management were all cloaked in language of personal responsibility. As a result, my faith took on a hyper-individualistic quality. Not only did I have Jesus as my *personal* Lord and Savior; I did *personal* devotions (and I felt incredibly guilty if I skipped them). My personal faith led to a preoccupation with myself and my own righteousness, or lack thereof. My faith had grown inward into a kind of spiritual narcissism. I had become as self-centered in my pursuit of God as I had been in my pursuit of self-indulgence. A fixation on my personal piety kept me from looking outward.

Although I had a moral conscience, I had not yet developed a social conscience. A social conscience moves us to care as deeply about the world as we do about ourselves. Martin Luther King said, "An individual has not started to live until [they] rise above [their] narrow, individualistic concerns to the broader concerns of humanity."[4] The broader concerns of humanity are the substance of a social conscience. A quote often attributed to Mother Teresa says it like this: "The problem with the world is that we draw the circle of family too small." The pivot toward solidarity is a pivot to widen our concern beyond that of ourselves and our family, culture, and nation until, eventually, everyone is included.

My social conscience developed exponentially when I moved to a big city and took time to enter into relationship with my neighbors. Choosing to broaden my social world opened my eyes, my heart, my faith, my politics, and my checkbook. My eyes were opened to systems of inequality. Living in the city and driving by underfunded schools, overcrowded prisons, and abandoned manufacturing warehouses, I could no longer ignore the reality of social forces on the lives of people around me. Bumping up against people from different cultures and backgrounds opened my heart to the beauty of diversity. I realized my cultural and theological perspectives were limited by growing up in segregated spaces and were enhanced by hearing other perspectives. The center of my faith shifted from self-centeredness to a commitment to solidarity and justice.

I began to notice that most of Scripture is written to communities, not individuals. The apostle Paul described the body of Christ as a diverse community of solidarity, not a clubhouse for homogenous individuals (1 Corinthians 12:21-26). My politics became less about how I could preserve my own interests and more about how I could defend the rights and interests of others who did not have the same access and privileges that I enjoyed. Even my financial habits changed. I realized that my frugality was actually a function of "personal responsibility" and kept me from being more generous with those who didn't have the same opportunities

---

4. Coretta Scott King, comp., *The Words of Martin Luther King, Jr.* (New York: William Morrow Publishing, 2011), 3. Martin Luther King used this quote or variations of it in many sermons and speeches.

and resources as me. Being fiscally responsible and saving money for the future is important, but if we are only occupied with our own future, then we have not yet developed a social conscience. A social conscience helps us develop the art of sharing so that everyone has enough. The shift to solidarity is a beautiful movement toward love, relationship, mutuality, generosity, and justice.

The shift to solidarity is essential, because collective self-centeredness can have a negative wide-scale effect on economically vulnerable communities. Take gentrification, which is happening in cities across the country. Back in 2005, my neighborhood started to show signs of gentrification. A movie theater, a name-brand grocery store, and even a Starbucks popped up in the same shopping mall. Developers started buying up apartment buildings and evicting longtime residents to create luxury condos and attract higher-income clientele. Fears were high among African American residents who had called North Lawndale home for generations. Since 1950, the neighborhood had seen a population loss of around seventy thousand people due to white flight. The creation of the suburbs after World War II had made it possible for white families to move away from neighborhoods like North Lawndale, which were becoming home for Blacks who came up from the South during the Great Migration.[5] For white families, the long commute from the suburbs to the city, where many still worked, was a small price to pay for the luxuries of single-family homes, brand-new appliances, spacious yards, reliable garbage pickup, quality schools, and well-policed streets.

Ironically, now the neighborhood was being positioned to entice white professionals back into the neighborhood—but by pricing out longtime residents, the trend was to the detriment of the existing community. My wife and I, both of us white, had moved into North Lawndale to live in solidarity with neighbors. But because of fears associated with gentrification, we had to prove that we

5. For more on the Great Migration, see Isabel Wilkerson, *The Warmth of Other Suns: The Epic Story of America's Great Migration* (New York: Vintage, 2011). For a detailed account of housing discrimination related to white flight in North Lawndale, see Beryl Satter, *Family Properties: Race, Real Estate, and Exploitation of Black Urban America* (New York: Metropolitan, 2009).

were coming into the neighborhood not strictly for our own benefit but rather to be part of the struggles of the community. In order to differentiate ourselves from the larger pattern of gentrification, we realized we had to pivot from self-centeredness to solidarity. This meant we couldn't think solely about our own economic self-interest but had to think about the common good.

Self-interest drove white flight, and it now drives gentrification. If we only think about what is good for us, we may inadvertently perpetuate injustice and pain for other people. Self-centeredness would have isolated us from our neighbors. Instead, we worked to build trust. We volunteered in the community, we mentored youth, my wife gardened, and we actively tried to put the interest of the neighborhood ahead of our own. Still, self-centeredness creeps in fast. Checking our own self-interest and reflecting on its impact on others can be tiring, but it's necessary. It's also an ongoing process. Solidarity is a choice to consider others in our decision-making. Solidarity means recognizing that pursuing naked self-interest is at the root of so much oppression.

A couple of years after the gentrifying trend in our neighborhood began, the housing market crashed. The movie theater, grocery store, and Starbucks closed, and the developers moved out and moved on. Many houses went into foreclosure and are still boarded up today. We are still here living alongside our neighbors, trying to resist the forces of self-centeredness in our hearts and in the systems that govern our world.

I do not know the definitive moment the pivot to solidarity happened, but I remember preaching at a multiracial church in Atlanta about some of the struggles that our community in Chicago was facing. In the sermon, I talked about how our community was experiencing a host of issues, including violence, mass incarceration, and environmental pollution. I shared stories from Scripture and from my community that showed how our faith provides resources for resistance and endurance in the struggle for justice (essentially I was talking about soul force).

At the end of the service, an African American friend of mine came up to me and said that one word stood out to her from my sermon. I was intrigued, and I asked her which one. "Every time you talked about your neighborhood you said 'our,'" she told me.

It wasn't my enthusiastic preaching or my deep theological points that had made the biggest impact. It was that the struggle of the community had become my own. She gave witness to the shift that had happened in me, from *I* to *we*. Before then, I had not thought about how important the word *our* can be. It made me think about the significance of the Lord's Prayer starting out with "Our Father." Right there, Jesus was training his disciples to see their relationship with God as connected to, not separated or segregated from, their brothers and sisters. He was calling them into community and communion with one another, as well as into relationship with him. In the kingdom of God, there is no *us* versus *them*. There's only *we* and *our*.

THREE EXPRESSIONS OF SOLIDARITY

Our friend Rediet Mulugeta is a deep soul who understands the profound beauty that solidarity brings to ourselves and others. Her family came to the United States from Ethiopia when she was five years old. Her experience of navigating different cultures and spaces has given her an appreciation for the ways humanity is tied together, as Martin Luther King said, "in a single garment of destiny."[6] She has identified for us three powerful expressions of solidarity that help us realize our interrelatedness with one another.[7]

I see you: Dignity

In 2010, Mulugeta traveled to Rwanda with five other college students. There she listened to and learned from the most resilient people she had ever encountered. Even now, eight years later, she told us, she finds herself returning to their stories, which portray endurance and what it means to embody hope amid the unfathomable daily realities of life after trauma.

---

6. Martin Luther King Jr., "Letter from a Birmingham Jail," chap. 5 in *Why We Can't Wait* (Boston: Beacon Press, 2010), 87. First published 1964.

7. We are indebted to Rediet Mulugeta for this threefold framework for solidarity. The *we* in this section represents our collective we, illustrating the solidarity with which the three of us also do life together.

One afternoon, she and the other students found themselves sitting with more than forty women who gather frequently in the church to share their burdens with one another to find comfort and healing. She met Odette, a widow of the 1994 genocide, who committed herself to sharing her story to help other women who survived the genocide to find healing. Odette calls this group Wrira, which means "don't cry" in Kinyarwanda. This sacred space was created for other women to listen, mourn, weep, and lament the brokenness that swept over Rwanda. It was intended to move women who once felt isolated in their grief toward community, and to remind them that they are seen and they are worthy of healing.

Through this experience, Mulugeta learned that the reconciliation process starts when we recognize the dignity and humanity in each person. Each woman had a story of pain that was her own, and each woman was given the space to share and be reminded that she was seen and loved. As each shared her pain, they together moved toward healing. They endured.

I love you: Proximity and presence

The sacred life stories, like the ones Mulugeta heard in Rwanda, are testimonials that endurance and resilience are a result of envisioning the world as it should be, even while in the wilderness. This vision flourishes when we pursue it together. All throughout Scripture, we are guided to "provoke one another to love and good deeds" (Hebrews 10:24). When we do this, we call one another near (proximity) and invite others into a sacred space with us (presence). Proximity moves us away from cheap compassion, which doesn't cost us anything, and toward true compassion, which guides us to walk beside one another through the ordinary and mundane aspects of life.

Like the women in Rwanda, we move toward hope and healing because of those who get close and create sacred space to gently welcome and be present to our pain. These past couple of years, there have been moments where we have been overcome with deep grief because of the violence against Black and brown bodies. When the feelings become too familiar and the words so few, there are moments in which the grief leads us to wrestle with our worth within this society. In these moments, it is our people who remind us that we are worthy of love as they make themselves available and choose to be actively present with us in the pain. They've taught us about a long-lasting love, one that gives hope. They've moved us toward love, and seeking more of it.

They've done this with great patience, love, and care that has led us to find strength and purpose. By getting close and being present to pain, we are reminded that we are worthy of love and belonging. This is what spurs us toward love and gives us endurance to pursue beloved community.

You belong: Community

Love is patient. It does not rush. It does not fix. It gives space for the Spirit to heal and restore. It moves us as close as we can get to the pain and suffering of our brothers and sisters. It teaches us to sit in the wilderness with one another. We believe that this type of compassionate love is found in community. Henri Nouwen writes that as we stay rooted in God's vision for our world, we become "compassionate people, deeply aware of our solidarity in brokenness with all of humanity."[8]

One aspect of solidarity is the willingness to see all life as sacred and worthy of love and belonging. We're reminded that we belong by recognizing that when one part of the body hurts, we all hurt. When one part of the body weeps, we all weep. It is in beloved community that we find the endurance to identify the false selves that keep us bound to the brokenness of the world. In community we may strive toward our true self, which is bound up in God's promises of healing and restoration.

"I've noticed that endurance is not found in isolation, but rooted in relationships and community," Mulugeta told us.

> For this reason, I purposefully surround myself with people who have transformed how I see, engage, and be with others in a way that gives me purpose. As we enter into the suffering and pain of our brothers and sisters together, we find ways to endure toward

---

8. Henri J. M. Nouwen, *The Way of the Heart* (San Francisco: HarperCollins, 1981), 40.

hope. We find ways to see the world as it is, and collectively move toward the world as it should be. When we remind one another that we are seen, that we are loved, and that we belong, somewhere along the way, we interweave our stories and find ways to carry one another forward toward beloved community.

We continue to invest in movements toward justice and love because we believe that we can never be what we ought to be until our stories are woven with the stories of our neighbors. Community is the place where we are reminded that we are seen, we are loved, and we belong. This is how we endure: through the solidarity of beloved community.

Solidarity is a journey, not a destination. This is why pivots are more productive than arrivals. If we have been unconsciously programmed in one way most of our lives, it will not be abnormal to occasionally (or even frequently!) slip back into old patterns of thinking or indoctrination.

Pivots provide opportunities to be fastidiously conscious—not self-defeating. Instead of denying, justifying, or defending our habits, we can pivot, allowing for necessary tweaks as we go. By pivoting, we can move toward beloved community and participate in a transformational movement.

SOUL FORCE STORY

From self-centeredness to solidarity

Bernadette Arthur

I grew up attending church services. Some of my earliest memories are of attending church services that were located anywhere from high school auditoriums to stained-glass-windowed sanctuaries. I remember begging my mother to use the restroom so I could have a three-minute reprieve from a five-hour service to slide down the empty high school corridors in my white stockinged feet. I also remember that if I lost track of the time, my mother would come looking for me.

From church I learned the art of public speaking and was encouraged by the rousing amens from my "aunties" and "uncles" in the pews in front of me. From church I learned that I was not an island and that I belonged to a wider cultural and spiritual community.

In recent years, it's this last lesson that I've come to see as invaluable and formative to who I am as an Afro-Caribbean Canadian woman. As an adult engaged in the ministry of racial justice and reconciliation in a denomination that is predominantly white, I can appreciate the rich cultural and spiritual roots of the institution. Much like the Caribbean churches that I attended growing up, the immigrant pioneers of this denomination sought refuge from the unfamiliarity and hostility of their wider society by forming spiritual communities that allowed them to maintain and foster their vibrant cultural heritage. What differs about the experiences of these cultural groups is that as time progressed, the ethnic identity of one of the immigrant communities became less of an anomaly to the wider culture, and they began to fully reap the benefits and privileges of their racial identity.

Whether asked for or not, whiteness remains a social construct that garners real unearned privilege and power in Canadian society. Thus, white congregants are challenged to be like Christ and self-empty. The challenge I've come against in my ministry work is how to invite and challenge white Canadian churches to participate in the redemptive work of redistribution of power and wealth, developing the practice of racial justice and reconciliation.

As a ministry leader, I invite and challenge my white brothers and sisters into a journey of self-emptying for the sake of the creation of authentic and restorative places of belonging. I've prayed and cried and struggled over exactly how to do this work of inviting and challenging. I have decided to do what I saw Jesus do: create space for people to dialogue over truths and a meal. This has proven to be an effective way for people to think about what needs to be unlearned so that greater solidarity can be achieved both within and outside the body of Christ.

I invited several trusted white brothers and sisters to embark on a minimum six-month journey of discovery and community with members of their racial community: to sit for a couple of hours a month to talk openly and honestly about racism in Canada and the church. They specifically focused on processing the ways that the image of God has been distorted in them because of their inheritance of whiteness. I am unable to share these stories of movement and transformation because they are not my stories. However, I'm told that these communities have slowly developed into spaces where authenticity, vulnerability, and solidarity abound. Community members are grateful to have a safe space to process without fear of offense, and they are eager to talk about a topic that for many of them has been taboo.

I asked Danielle Steenwyk-Rowaan, a respected colleague, friend, and facilitator, to share the effect that gathering in these communities has had on her and her fellow community members. "For the past four months, I've led a little group of white people who have an inkling that we have privilege and don't know what to do about it," she told me.

> We've done some hard listening to the voices of people of color. We've wrestled with intent versus impact and the idea that even if we don't really understand why a comment is offensive to a person of color, they get to decide what's offensive to them, even if that decision varies among people of color. This idea made us feel a bit destabilized (and that fact alone reveals our privilege yet again). We've called ourselves back over and over again to the example of Jesus, who, unlike us, had every right to his privilege and yet emptied himself of his privilege in order to be in reconciled relationships with us (see Philippians 2). I've been grateful for people in our group who grew up with significant money stress in their homes and yet see that their whiteness gives them privilege—this work of encountering our privilege is complex, hard work!

The experiences of Steenwyk-Rowaan and her group members are not atypical. I frequently hear of how community group members are doing things that they would not have done before for the sake of shifting power and creating space for people of color. The journey is not yet over, but even in its infancy stages, it is apparent that these community groups have created a space that challenges the characteristics of whiteness and allows people to incrementally move toward solidarity with those in their community who are racially different from themselves.

SOUL FORCE PIVOT POINTS

Take a chance on one another

While self-preservation may protect us from pain, it also can keep us from deep relationships with people. What keeps you from opening yourself up? What do you gain from self-preservation? What do you miss out on?

Trust each other

Trust is one of the most important natural resources. Trust is the fabric of community and relationship. Solidarity is formed by building trust. Instead of seeking to save, fix, or control spaces where people are hurting, how can you build trust?

Relinquish the need to control everything

Why do we have a need to control? What would it look like to give up control? What makes that scary?

Resist the urge to hoard

How much is enough? What are needs and what are wants? Why is it hard to let go? What was given to you for you, and what was *entrusted* to you to give to someone else? What can you live without?

Share our resources

Do you find it difficult to share? What holds you back? What do you have in excess that others need? How can you open up your resources, networks, and finances to support others?

Develop a social conscience

How can you broaden your concern for individuals, families, and communities beyond yourself? How open are your heart, faith, politics, and checkbook to people who are on margins of society?

Truly know with whom we are standing in solidarity

What invitations have you received to enter into the struggle of others? How did you respond? What people or struggles have you felt drawn to learn more about? What would it look like for you to get closer?

Give more than just money, as in charity or the purchase of a ticket. Go beyond imagining to enacting

What are you willing to give up or lose to move from self-centeredness to solidarity? How do you expect to be transformed by living in solidarity?

_____

PIVOT 3 MANTRA

I am because we are.

Pivot 4

FROM HURT TO HOPE

"Still I'll rise."
—MAYA ANGELOU

Hurt takes many forms, and our hearts and minds can take a long time to unravel and heal. Past and present hurts can block the flow of soul force. Our emotions become stopped up, like clogged pipes, by confusion, pain, anger, hatred, and resentment, in ways that become incapacitating.

This chapter takes a deeper look into the hurt we all carry, so that we can experience the healing and hope on the other side. James Baldwin said, "Not everything that is faced can be changed, but nothing can be changed until it is faced."[1] Until we face our hurt, we cannot fully experience healing and hope. Soul force isn't a Band-Aid, a cheery optimism to medicate ourselves from reality. Soul force brings us face-to-face with pain—our own and others'—so that we can experience the healing power of truth and love. Soul force builds our capacity for nonviolent resistance and hope-filled resilience. Hope reminds us that hurt does not have to have the final word in our story.

---

1. James Baldwin, "As Much Truth as One Can Bear," *New York Times Book Review*, January 14, 1962; republished in *The Cross of Redemption: Uncollected Writings*, ed. Randall Kenan (New York: Vintage, 2011), 42.

Of all the pivots we discuss in this book, this pivot may take the most courage, but it can also be the most transformational.

THE SECRECY AND VULNERABILITY OF HURT

We all experience hurt, and hurt can leave a long-lasting mark on our souls. Hurt can cause us to regress in our journey of transformation. Hurt can cause us to retreat back into fear, create barriers of protectionism, and return to a self-centered orientation that keeps us further isolated from others. What makes hurt so devastating is its secretive nature. We may carry deep pain and heaviness without anyone knowing. On the outside, we can appear to have it all together. We can be successful in our profession and even lifted up on a pedestal by others while inside we are dying and holding deep hurts.

Truth be told, this chapter was the hardest for me (Reesheda) to write. On top of whatever the hurt is in my life and work, I have been indoctrinated, as a Black woman, to maintain the secrecy of my hurt, for a number of reasons. Mostly people don't want to hear it. People say, "I'm tired of talking about race"; "I'm tired of talking about gender equity"; "You make me uncomfortable." Or I don't say anything because I've been well trained that some feelings should remain unvoiced, so I keep my pain to myself. I've been taught to protect white people and to protect the emotional fragility of men, so I just know not to talk about my pain. As a Black person, woman, and mother, I was taught early that my role is to maintain the safety or comfort of everyone else. For those of us in these roles, there's little room to talk about what's paining us.

History tells me that to talk about my hurt is to create more hurt for myself. If I'm fully transparent about what's hurting me, then I open myself up to backlash from the power structure that is creating pain for me. Usually those with more power than me in a situation do not take a posture of receptivity. They are usually defensive, and in an effort to disengage with their pain, they create more pain for me by disengaging from relationship with me, terminating my role, or cutting off my funding. If I name the things they do that hurt me, they don't understand why I am saying these things to them; it makes them uncomfortable; and it could end up getting me fired or otherwise censured. Instead of being seen as someone who is hurting, I am seen as someone who is disrespecting the hierarchy and stepping out of my designated place. The articulation of my hurt often creates more pain for me. By default, it makes me not even want to acknowledge it.

"YET DO I MARVEL"

The words of African American poet Countee Cullen in the poem "Yet Do I Marvel" express the tensions that exist between hurt and hope in our world. The poem depicts a frustrated narrator who is dealing with the profundities of God—a speaker who, while declaring the goodness of the Lord, and while proclaiming his faith in the Almighty, is perplexed by God's decision to allow, for example, the torture of Tantalus and the never-ending vexation of Sisyphus. The narrator marvels at a God who has suffered him the perils of being Black in America in the 1920s, when this poem was penned—and then expected him to sing and write. "Yet do I marvel at this curious thing: To make a poet black and bid him sing!"[2]

Yet does he marvel! And haven't you been there? Haven't you at some point in your life looked at a situation or the circumstances of a loved one and marveled at the doings of the Lord? Haven't you marveled at how or why God has allowed for calamities of the heart, vexations of the mind, and quandaries of the soul? Have you not ever looked at what some sweet, kind person was enduring and wondered, "Why her?" or "Why him?" Indeed, haven't you ever wondered why God has allowed for some adversity in your own life, to which you have responded, "Why me?"

A THEODICY OF HURT: WHY DOES GOD ALLOW IT?

Why does God allow evil? This is a question we all wrestle with on a very deep level. Theologians have come up with their own theodicies—explanations for why a good God would allow evil and suffering in the world. We do not claim to fully know this answer, but we do know this: God is big enough to carry all the hurt that God allows to exist in the world.

2. Countee Cullen, "Yet Do I Marvel," in *Color* (New York: Harper, 1925).

This is a scary thing to write, but we believe it's true. If we say it, then that means God is big enough to hold slavery, war, mass incarceration, genocide, abuse, and all the other hurtful things that exist in the world. We believe God is big enough to hold it all.

The difficult thing is this: we don't want this belief to be heard by anyone as an excuse to say, "I don't have to do anything, because God is big enough to hold it." There's a tension here. Yes, God is big enough to hold the hurt. But God also wants to work in and through us to heal the hurt.

We believe that God allows hurt because God knows that suffering is the very thing that most ignites us to love, live, collaborate, transform, and commune with one another. Sadly, we are not always inspired to such things from a space of rest and peace. We are not motivated by the comforts of life to go and respond to hurt and pain and suffering. It's only *out* of hurt and pain and suffering that we are mobilized to do something with it.

We can't talk about a pivot from hurt to hope without naming our theodicy: our belief that God allows hurt because God knows how we're wired. Could it be that the whole reason hurt exists is that we can't get inspired to action without it? Because God is big enough to hold the hurt that God allows, because God wants us to be in loving, peaceful, and transformative community with one another, and because God knows hurt is what moves us to act in love: for all these reasons, God allows pain to exist.

That is a tough pill to swallow. We're not ready to say that hurt is the only thing that inspires us to act for change—although every day both of us do, in fact, move and act because of the hurt we see in the world. So much of what we both do in our work is in response to hurt. We are writing this book in response to hurt in the world. If pain didn't exist, would we be in community with each other? We simply can't talk about hope without naming these tensions.

A PERSONAL STORY OF HURT AND HOPE

As a child, I (Reesheda) was an inquisitive latchkey daughter of a "strong Black woman." My mom did all that she could—including the seemingly impossible—to raise me with love and support.

Nevertheless, the unyielding institutionalized systems designed to promote insecurity, low self-esteem, and a need for validation—particularly for young female children of color—worked like a charm, and I was a teenage mom by the age of fifteen. I had been a mostly compliant honors student up until then, so the news of my pregnancy created a surge of shock and disappointment throughout my family. Today I have only vague memories of the painful details of this experience, as so much beauty and joy has come in the twenty-eight years since then.

I do remember three particular instances, however, that were connected with this experience and that brought me deep pain: telling my mother that I was pregnant; enduring labor and delivery with no medication; and receiving an anonymous letter from someone affiliated with my high school, attempting to shame me for having publicly received academic accolades while I was a teenage mom. These three moments still produce pangs of remorse and regret—not for having had my daughter, but for the conditions in which her glorious arrival occurred.

A meandering depression flitted in and out of me those forty weeks, although the shame that accompanied my sadness led me to minimize the impact of it. To say that the hurt was heavy is an understatement. I spent a great deal of my life in and after that season trying to understand why God had allowed me to become pregnant. I was a "good girl." There were other girls behaving more egregiously than I ever had, and they seemed to be "getting away" with everything. Throughout my life, other events had made me wonder why God had allowed them to happen, and in all those cases, I eventually had surmised a "good reason" for why each had occurred. But this experience? I simply could not come to terms with it.

Then one day, during my very late thirties, it finally hit me. I was nearly turning forty, and as is often the case when experiencing a milestone birthday, I was reflecting on my life and all that I had experienced. I remembered the reasons that I had become a teacher. As a young mother, I had wanted to be sure that I would be home in the summers when my daughter was home. More significantly, I had wanted to educate her well, and I had figured that studying to become a teacher would equip me to ensure that my daughter would receive the best possible education. I thought about how I had chosen to live in particular neighborhoods, and how I had developed affiliations with very specific church communities according to what would be best for my daughter. I considered how I had delved into social justice and equity-based work, because I wanted to ensure the best possible future for my daughter and her peers.

Thus I was almost forty years old before I realized that every good, real, and right choice I had made since birthing my daughter had come to me as a result of her existence! My entire adulthood had been curated and designed with her in mind. This realization caused me to overflow with hopefulness and joy at what God had produced out of one of the most hurtful times of my life. Before this epiphany I had not realized how much hope could be born (both literally and metaphorically) out of that which was originally hurtful.

And so I received three gifts: the beautiful journey that had become my life; the realization of hope born out of hurt; and of course, my amazingly brilliant daughter, Datrianna, a perpetual source of hope, who is already kicking life in the seat of the pants!

HURT IS A BENEFACTOR OF HOPE

From this journey, I have learned that hurt is sometimes the benefactor of hope—if we can see our way through to the other side of the circumstances creating our discomfort. This is not an attempt to coerce anyone to stay in circumstances that are life threatening or violent. Rather, it is to say that life will inevitably render some pain, challenge, and discomfort. When it does, if we can tap into soul force, there may also be some fodder for growth, strength, and supplication. We can receive difficult events as a means for transformation for ourselves and our communities.

Even as you read this text, some of you might be marveling and wondering at what God has given you to carry and birth. Perhaps God has given it to you at a time and in a place and circumstances

that seem painful to bear. You might be asking what God is up to
. . . you might yet marvel. There is a simple answer for all of this:
God loves us so much that God sometimes gives us what I refer to
as "the opportunity in the affliction."

Now, I know you are wondering: How can opportunity be in
an affliction, and why you would ever call it a gift from God?

As you consider your circumstances, reflect on the story I just
shared, reflect on other challenging times in your life, and recall
how you emerged from those experiences. The ways out may vary,
but one thing is for certain: transcending hurt will always require
soul force. It will always require you to tap into that part of you
that holds the most wisdom, the most ability to discern and to
experience the greatest power that resides within you. Your soul
force is what makes you a conqueror. Soul force is what makes
you look back at circumstances that have plagued you, and soul
force makes you ask yourself how you ever got over the pain or
the struggle, because you knew that it was not within your own
strength, power, or might. What was required was beyond your
capacity. Soul force affords us all the strength and power to do the
otherwise unthinkable, unimaginable, and seemingly unattainable.

Had you told me twenty-eight years ago that I would raise a
daughter as incredible as the one I have today, I would probably
have said that *both* she and I were doomed! Statistics show that
teenage single moms of color and their children do not typically
fare well. But by faith, I was able to mine the reservoirs within my
soul—the power that God had put there for such a time as the
one I was experiencing. Time and time again, I have gone back to
that reservoir, and each time it has been full enough for me to be
replenished for the challenging times ahead. I have revisited the
reservoir of soul force more times than I can count, so I can look
back and see the ways that hurt has been restored to hopefulness
in my life and in the lives of those in my community.

To be clear, while I celebrate the ways my hurt has been transformed into hope, it is also important to note that the road to transformation is not usually an easy one. We must take certain steps to
realize holistic transformation in ourselves and our communities.

FIVE SOUL FORCE PRACTICES FOR HEALING

Through our own journeys and by listening to other people with whom we have walked, we have identified five soul force practices for healing. These practices have the power to transform hurt to hope. These are not meant to be formulaic or prescriptive, but they can serve as signposts, pointing us to the way of healing and hope.

1. Care for trauma

In the work we do, we see many types of trauma. The emotional trauma of stress, anxiety, and depression, and the physical trauma of abuse, food insecurity, and violence: these all affect people's ability to function in all the areas of their life. Trauma creates added burdens to life that weigh heavy on the soul and create great strain. If we want to see people thrive, we have to address the underlying trauma and woundedness that we all carry, sometimes deep under the surface. To expect people to thrive in life without addressing the underlying trauma in their hearts and environment is like expecting someone with a broken leg to run a marathon. It doesn't matter how much you apply or push yourself, you are only going to do more damage until you give yourself the time, space, and support needed to heal. Likewise, we cannot live abundant lives if we don't first address our own trauma, hurt, and emotional woundedness.

When I (Shawn) entered into the pain of solidarity with my community, I was eager to engage the brokenness of the city. I was less prepared to confront my own brokenness. My middle-class upbringing, which shielded me from a lot of the indignities and injustices my neighbors have experienced, could not completely shield me from the traumas that living in a neighborhood of concentrated poverty provokes. The rawness of the city exposed cracks in my own life. Growing up in white culture, in which silence rather than confrontation was the norm, I had not developed my voice to name hurt or speak out about injustice. Being a pastor's kid, I also didn't feel that I could voice my pain without it reflecting badly on our family's ministry. So instead of dealing with my pain, I stuffed it down inside and kept quiet. The ubiquity and intensity of the pain in the city made it impossible to ignore my own emotions and stay silent in the face of them. I slowly learned to open up and express the full range of emotions. Protesting injustice alongside my community helped me find my voice and learn how to advocate for myself as well as my community.

Secondary traumatic stress disorder (STSD), also referred to as compassion fatigue, is a lesser-known form of trauma that can affect people, such as pastors and counselors and activists, who are caring for victims of trauma. Secondary trauma occurs when we are affected vicariously or indirectly by the trauma of others. As pastor Jerry Gernander writes, "The symptoms of a person suffering primary traumatic stress disorder at every stage are identical to the symptoms of a person suffering secondary traumatic stress disorder."[3] When we come into contact with the traumatized, marginalized, and hurting, we are susceptible to suffering similar trauma. In fact, with viral videos and the 24/7 news cycle, many of us are in a constant state of secondary trauma.

Instead of trivializing, ignoring, or numbing our feelings, we need to acknowledge the pain, bring our traumas to light, and enter the road of recovery. Talking with a pastor, coach, or mental health counselor about our past and our pain can provide us with support and tools for dealing with trauma in healthy ways. Trauma care takes our pain seriously and allows us to bring our hurts and the hurts of others into a dynamic process of healing.

2. Express righteous indignation

The second practice involves acknowledging and directing our anger. It's been said, "If you're not outraged, you're not paying attention." Much injustice in our world elicits our anger. The apostle Paul says, "Be angry but do not sin" (Ephesians 4:26). But Scripture doesn't say to ignore or deny your anger. Even Jesus, in a moment of anger, got righteously indignant at the exploitation of the poor happening outside the temple of God. He flipped tables and drove out the money changers with a whip (see Matthew 21:12-13).

---

3. Jerry Gernander, "Compassion Fatigue: A Problem for Pastors" (presentation, ELS General Pastoral Conference, Bloomington, MN, October 1, 2014), http://issuesetc .org/wp-content/uploads/2014/10/Compassion-Fatigue-GPC-2014.pdf.

The fire of anger can be constructive or destructive. In his book *The Bush Was Blazing but Not Consumed*, Eric Law argues that fire has a dual purpose. Fire can purify and it can consume. Anger is like a fire, and our responsibility is to use the fire to purify (ourselves and others), not to harm. Law urges us to keep the fire holy. When God is present in the midst of the fire, then the fire can burn but not consume.[4] Let the anger drive out our own selfish motives and complicity with injustice. Let the anger move us toward the God who shares our anger at injustice and suffering. Let the anger move us from apathy into righteous indignation and action. The prophet Isaiah states, "For I the Lord love justice, I hate robbery and wrongdoing" (Isaiah 61:8). Therefore, we know that God is asking us not to give up our anger but to transform it into a nonviolent force for love and justice.

Much like the fire metaphor in Law's book, suffering acts as a double-edged sword. When we know the anger of Christ, we also know his suffering. And while we know that some suffering is inevitable, we are not suggesting that anyone stay in a place, relationship, or culture of abuse. All too often, concepts of anger, righteousness, and suffering have themselves been manipulated under the guise of faith to foster subjugation, exploitation, and enslavement. We want to be clear that we are not condoning such false ideology and theology. Rather, we encourage you to monitor and discern your conditions of suffering so that you are protected from a hazardous environment.

We have noticed that many people involved in social justice work—ourselves included—have experienced hurt in their lives. Our work to make the world right often comes from a desire to see the woundedness in our own lives made right. Our understanding of power comes from our own experiences as victims of abuses of power. The work of justice includes both our healing and the healing of the world. Justice is not only about fighting for better systems or policies; it's about longing for and seeking healing for everything that is broken.

---

4. Eric Law, *The Bush Was Blazing but Not Consumed* (St. Louis: Chalice Press, 1996), 18–25.

When we address the world's brokenness but neglect our own, hate, unrighteous anger, and resentment can build up, causing more damage to ourselves. The work of justice requires ridding ourselves and our society of evil, hate, and violence by pursuing the healing and health of everyone.

3. Lament injustice

One of our nonviolent weapons and spiritual practices is lament. Lament gives an outlet for anger, pain, and disappointment without trivializing or minimizing them. Soong-Chan Rah, in his book *Prophetic Lament*, writes that "lament recognizes the struggles of life and cries out for justice against existing injustices. The status quo is not to be celebrated but instead must be challenged."[5]

Sometimes we want to move quickly to solutions, but we have to first allow ourselves to be upset when injustice and tragedy happen. We have to learn to lament.

After witnessing the barrage of viral videos and hashtags of Black bodies strung across our screens, Reesheda reached out to me (Shawn) and some others. She felt moved to provide space for people of color and allies across Chicago to come together and grieve the onslaught of racial injustice. Overwhelmed with the heavy realities of anguish and pain, she shared an idea for organizing a day of bereavement and lament.

We wanted to have a space for people who might not be able to publicly grieve at their workplace or church. We needed to acknowledge the pain that so many of us were feeling. Amid pushbacks and social media arguments, what was missing were spaces to allow ourselves to weep, mourn, and grieve.

So it was that we gathered a group of friends in a public park in the heart of downtown Chicago. It was a somber night among friends, a place to be okay with not being okay. We were invited to share a song, poem, or lament without judgment. Anger was allowed, and tears were welcomed.

---

5. Soong-Chan Rah, *Prophetic Lament: A Call for Justice in Troubled Times* (Downers Grove, IL: InterVarsity Press, 2015), 23.

A teenager shared a song and broke down because of a recent tragedy in which a classmate was brutally killed by other students. I thought about the heaviness that this young generation is carrying. They are the first generation to grow up seeing death captured and disseminated on their television screens, cell phones, and social media pages.

We took time to light candles and pray over the twenty-six-page stack of names of the victims of violence in our city during the past year. We tried to enter into the pain being experienced by the families and loved ones of these victims, and we prayed for the neighborhoods where these incidents happened. We didn't solve any problems. We didn't trivialize the pain. We "let suffering speak," as brother Cornel West admonishes.[6] We came together to care for one another and let that be enough.

At the park that evening, I thought about the fact that many of my African American friends experience a double trauma: first of learning about these horrible tragedies, and then of *not* hearing their pastors, coworkers, and white friends talk about them at all. I realized my friends needed to hear me speak up, to say that their lives mattered. It wasn't enough to be upset or grieve privately; I needed to raise my voice publicly to name and renounce the injustices.

At the gathering on the day of bereavement, I shared a poem I wrote to express my feelings about many of the racial injustices that were happening and my disappointment with the lack of sensitivity and solidarity from many white people across the country and in our churches. Here's an excerpt from the poem:

"Give us your tired, huddled masses longing to be free"
and watch the life get choked out
Eric Garner still can't breathe
If protest is the language of the unheard
then Black Lives Matter is the spoken word

6. Cornel West, "A World of Ideas," *The Cornel West Reader* (New York: Basic Civitas, 1999), 294. West credits Theodor Adorno with the origin of this idea in the book *Negative Dialectics*: "The need to lend a voice to suffering is a condition of all truth." Theodor W. Adorno, *Negative Dialectics*, trans. E. B. Ashton (New York: Routledge, 2004), 17. First English translation published 1973.

Don't you know silence is consent?
Democracy doesn't work without dissent.

"Hands up, don't shoot!"
Dead bodies on the street still not proof?
How long will justice delay?
For Trayvon, Laquan, Tamir, and Freddie Gray
Politicians pandering, it's all white noise
Whatcha gonna do to end the deaths of Black boys?

Talk is cheap
don't believe your own chatter
You say, "justice for all"
but you can't even say "Black lives matter!"
"No Justice, No Peace.
No Justice. No Peace."
You'd say the same if it was your child's blood on the streets.

This poem was a form of lament, but it was also a protest against white denial in the face of Black suffering. Lament involves expressing uncomfortable truths and remembering pain that others so easily forget or try to ignore.

4. Engage the process of forgiveness

Forgiveness is one of the most sacred and complex spiritual practices. After the 2015 church massacre in Charleston, South Carolina, there was a lot of debate over the role of forgiveness. Members at Emanuel African Methodist Episcopal Church sent shockwaves around the nation when they extended forgiveness to the perpetrator who had gunned down their sisters and brothers during a Bible study. These followers of Jesus offered a very tangible example of the power of forgiveness. Some within the African American and activist communities pushed back, questioning whether the burden of forgiveness should always rest on the shoulders of Black folks.

Pastor Tyshawn Gardner, a friend and co-laborer in the struggle for racial justice, wrote a very insightful piece on the importance of understanding forgiveness as a process that should not be imposed on those who have experienced abuse or injustice. He gave us permission to share this from his Facebook page:

A demand of unparalleled proportions is placed on the shoulders of Black Christians who have endured racial atrocities in this country: forgiveness. Christians are often asked or even expected to forgive the racial atrocities perpetrated against us with jet-like speed. However, our haste to "forgive" often reveals dangerous flaws in our theology; our belief in an unhealthy and unbiblical requirement of God to suppress our personal and communal anger, abuse, and hurt in exchange for a "ticket" into the pearly gates. We are willing to blindly forfeit the justice and righteousness of God on earth in exchange for the glories of heaven. "Thy kingdom come, thy will be done, on earth, as it is in heaven" presents a proper balance of expectation for the Christian. An either/or theology is improper. One must develop a healthy theology of forgiveness. At the core, our motivation to forgive is often rooted in both an unhealthy fear of God (to punish us if we don't forgive in a "timely" manner) and a nihilism that is anchored to our helplessness to confront the evil that caused the wounds. Until we take time to sit with our pain, anger, hurts and fear, *before* we run to "release" the perpetrators, we do neither them nor ourselves any good. True forgiveness cannot precede inner peace. The act of forgiveness can only transform the racist and the victim of racism when we allow the hurt of racism to be seen, heard, and felt. Hiding, covering, and rushing through our hurts transforms no one. One must realize that the interval between the occurrence of our wound and the act of forgiveness is a sacred space, not a hateful place. That is a time that we simply concede to the fact that we are mortals who need time and space to lament, to be angry, to be sad, and to verbally express our hurt, while we wrestle with our pain and process our hurt with a God who is able to wrest it all from our hands as he gives us permission to be at peace and let it go.

Forgiveness is a process and a personal journey. We should not feel coerced to forgive, or feel guilt or shame if we are not able to forgive within a certain time frame. Forgiveness is a choice, yes, but it is also a healing process. Our inability to forgive sometimes means there is more hurt to be unearthed and more healing still to be done. Ultimately, we cannot rush the healing process; we can only stay open to the process.

5. Wear down hate with love

In Romans, Paul urges the community of believers to not return evil for evil, but to "overcome evil with good" (Romans 12:21). One of the main enemies of soul force is hate. When we have been hurt, or when we see others in society being hurt, guarding against hate in our own souls is a challenge. Gandhi's philosophy of soul force originated as a nonviolent tactic and tool against violent oppression. The purpose of soul force as a nonviolent method is to return good for evil until the evildoer tires of evil.[7]

When Martin Luther King went up against white supremacy during the civil rights movement, he determined to not return hate with hate but to meet hate with love. In *Jesus and the Disinherited*, Howard Thurman, one of King's mentors, devotes a chapter to resisting hate. He describes Jesus' instruction to his disciples to love enemies and turn the other cheek, not just for the benefit of their enemy, but to preserve their own souls:

> Above and beyond all else it must be borne in mind that hatred tends to dry up the springs of creative thought in the life of the hater, so that his resourcefulness becomes completely focused on the negative aspects of his environment. The urgent needs of the personality for creative expression are starved to death. A man's horizon may become so completely dominated by the intense character of his hatred that there remains no creative residue in his mind and spirit to give to great ideas, to great concepts.[8]

It's been said that harboring hatred and resentment is like swallowing poison and expecting the other person to die. Hate is poison to the soul. Soul force—the alignment with love over hate, peace over violence, and faith over despair—preserves our own soul in the fight against evil. The ultimate victory of evil would be for us to mirror the evil and hatred of those who do violence to us. Soul force is about ridding our own soul of hatred even as

---

7. Louis Fischer, *Gandhi: His Life and Message for the World* (New York: Mentor, 1982), 35.

8. Howard Thurman, *Jesus and the Disinherited* (Boston: Beacon Press, 1996), 88. First published 1949.

we resist hatred, letting the force of love and mercy overcome the
drive within us for vengeance and retribution.

In a powerful appeal, Martin Luther King urged his supporters
to wear down hate through nonviolent resistance:

> To our most bitter opponents we say: "We shall match your
> capacity to inflict suffering by our capacity to endure suffer-
> ing. We shall meet your physical force with soul force. Do
> to us what you will, and we shall continue to love you. We
> cannot in good conscience obey your unjust laws, because
> non-co-operation with evil is as much a moral obligation as is
> co-operation with good. Throw us into jail, and we shall still
> love you. Send your hooded perpetrators of violence into our
> community at the midnight hour and beat us and leave us half
> dead, and we shall still love you. But be ye assured that we will
> wear you down by our capacity to suffer. One day we shall win
> freedom, but not only for ourselves. We shall so appeal to your
> heart and conscience that we shall win you in the process, and
> our victory will be a double victory."[9]

Caring for trauma, expressing righteous indignation, lamenting
injustice, engaging the process of forgiveness, and wearing down
hate with love: these are five sacred practices that have the power
to heal the soul and prepare the way for hope and resilience.

WE RISE: THE PIVOT TOWARD HOPE

I (Shawn) have felt overwhelmed by the trauma, suffering, and
injustice in my city and in the world. The steady feeling of despair
and dread has hovered over my heart and held me back from the
hope that I know in my mind is available to me. Simply put, I
have felt the heaviness of everything. The nonsense of the political news cycle. The disappointment in and frustration with other
Christians who misrepresent the faith. The pain of companioning
friends through their darkest moments. The trauma and violence
the young people in my neighborhood experience every day. It is
all too much.

But then I think of the cross.

---

9. Martin Luther King, *Strength to Love* (Philadelphia: Fortress Press, 1963), 54–55.

We often spiritualize the cross, and by doing so we lose sight of the fact that it was a traumatic event. The cross reveals the trauma of abuse, injustice, and structural violence. It exposes how violence and death so easily become culturally acceptable. The cross shows the insidious ways religion sells itself out for power and colludes with political forces to dehumanize people and institutionalize violence against the marginalized.

But the cross is also about resilience. Resilience is "the ability to become strong, healthy, and successful after something bad happens."[10] It means "adapting well in the face of adversity, trauma, tragedy, threats or significant sources of stress."[11]

Resilience is soul force. Resilience is the resurrection of Christ and the resistance of our neighbors to forces of death, hopelessness, and despair. Some of the most surprising and inspiring people are not those who have managed to avoid pain and suffering, but those who are still standing, praying, believing, and loving after facing the worst of human tragedy. Resilience is part of our kingdom formation, and it's developed by enduring and overcoming hardship.

Resilience is rising when the weight of the world is bearing down on us. We see the resilience of the resurrection every day we walk down our blocks. People are rising up and not letting fear and death have the last word. We believe in the power of the resurrection because we see God in the resilience of people in our communities. Everything we know about soul force is from living alongside neighbors and working shoulder to shoulder with community leaders who have had to demonstrate it over and over again. We know actual widows who fight injustice with the same tenacity as the widow in Jesus' parable of the unjust judge (Luke 18:1-8). We see the young Joshuas who are ready to hit the streets to march until the walls come down. We see everyday heroes who will never be publicly recognized saying yes to life and no to forces that aim to steal, kill, and destroy.

---

10. *Merriam-Webster Dictionary*, s.v. "resilience," accessed January 16, 2018, https://www.merriam-webster.com/dictionary/resilience.

11. "The Road to Resilience," APA, accessed January 9, 2018, http://www.apa.org/helpcenter/road-resilience.aspx.

Could it be that this resilience—this soul force—is further evidence of God's resurrection power at work in the world? After all, the apostle Paul writes, "If the Spirit of him who raised Jesus from the dead dwells in you, he who raised Christ from the dead will give life to your mortal bodies also through his Spirit that dwells in you" (Romans 8:11).

In this sense, the resurrection is not only something that happened two thousand years ago, but something that can give us power and life and strength every day. This is indeed reason for hope.

SOUL FORCE STORY
From hurt to hope

Lance Curley

Let me introduce myself in the Navajo way. First and foremost, I hope you see Jesus through me. My name is Lance Curly, my first clan is Towering House clan, which comes from my mom, and the second, I am born from the Mexican Clan, which is my dad. Then my paternal grandparents are Bitter Water Clan, and maternal grandparents are the Cliff Dwelling people. And this is what makes me a Navajo man.

I grew up on the Navajo Nation, an Indian reservation that officially encompasses twenty-five thousand square miles in northeastern Arizona, northwestern New Mexico, and southeastern Utah. When I was a baby, I didn't have a mom per se. She was there awhile, but she left my dad when I was a year old. I didn't think much about it. I would see her once in a while, and she would take me places, but we didn't have a relationship. You see a lot of single-parent households on the reservation, with moms raising a child alone. Usually it's the fathers who leave, or grandparents who end up raising the children because both parents are so young. I'd see families and think, "I'm not like that." Growing up in a house with a father and mother may be normal for other people, but that was not normal for us. As I grew up, I was raised primarily by my grandmother. She was the caretaker for most of us.

I didn't realize the impact my mom's absence would have on my life. I tried seeking that nurturing from other people. I started seeking relationships with the opposite sex. Most of those relationships ended the same way: the women left or cheated on me, which caused me to harbor more resentment, pain, and hatred for what my mom did to me. I continued to blame myself. I thought it was my fault she didn't love me or want me, which gave me lower self-esteem, drove me into depression, and produced thoughts of leaving or giving up on everything. I didn't want to end my life, but I wanted to give up on my dreams because I felt that nobody cared.

I had always looked up to my grandmother because she was the matriarch of the family and gave me hope that there was someone out there who cared. Her health eventually started to deteriorate. I always thought she'd be there for me. Her passing broke our family apart. Many family members, including me, turned to alcohol to deal with the pain, not knowing how to grieve properly. I started running away from God and distancing myself from friends, people from church, and mentors. People would ask how I was doing, and I'd pretend to be okay.

I went to Philadelphia to serve with Mission Year, and my city director, Ra Mendoza, pushed me to talk a lot and open up about who I was. Opening up to a group of people, people I hadn't known before, was very different. I had to trust God with my healing.

After going through this process of healing, I started to see what healthy relationships looked like from my mentor's family. I started to realize that I could have a family, and that there is such a thing as a healthy family. It opened my eyes to wanting to pursue helping people. I wanted to help my own Navajo community. I decided to go into social work because I realized there's a huge need and opportunity in the Native community in North America.

When I lived in Philadelphia and told people I was Native American, some said they didn't know Natives were still alive. So often we feel forgotten by society. When people do see Native culture, it's usually negative or stereotypical—as if we all live in tepees or hunt buffalo, when, in fact, we have our own history, identity, and culture. Each tribe is unique, with its own language, customs, laws, way of life, and unique history. We all have our own creation story of how we came to be.

When I left the reservation to go to Philadelphia, I was able to look at my tribe from a third-person perspective, which opened my eyes to the beauty of my culture and to the ways we have bought into lies.

Right now, my dream would be for Indigenous communities— not only my local community, but across North America—to be healthy communities. I'd like us to be forerunners bringing healing to this land, to this nation. I would also like to see young people empowered to take their place by not being afraid and by living free of oppression.

SOUL FORCE PIVOT POINTS

Allow the full range of human emotion

It's okay to feel what you feel. There are no bad emotions. Give yourself permission to feel the full range of human emotion. What emotions are you feeling? What makes you angry? What emotions do you struggle to acknowledge? Gather together with others, and lament in community. Host a day of bereavement to give space for people to voice their pain, anger, and hope for healing.

Address your wounds first

Seeking our own healing is not selfish or self-centered. There is no virtue in neglecting ourselves or suppressing our emotions. Our health is tied with the world's health. When we are healthy, we have more to offer the world. When the world is healthy, our health benefits.

Go to counseling

Have you experienced emotional or physical trauma? Have you talked with a counselor or mental health provider? What makes you hesitant about going to counseling?

Forgive but don't accept injustice

Where are you in the process of forgiveness? Do you find it easy or difficult to forgive? Give yourself permission to move slowly. Have you felt the freedom of forgiveness? Where do you still long for freedom?

When you heal, help someone else

We are all "wounded healers," as Henri Nouwen says.[12] Once we have experienced healing and hope, it is our responsibility and privilege to help others who are hurting. Our healing is for us, but it can also help people who are still in the depths of the pain.

Tell your story

Your story is powerful. When you feel ready, share your story with others. Richard Rohr talks about the authority of those who suffer. Those who have suffered carry a certain authority and expertise in that area. Telling your story not only builds courage within yourself; it emboldens others to tell their stories too.

PIVOT 4 MANTRA

I will rise up.

---

12. Henri J. M. Nouwen, *The Wounded Healer: Ministry in Contemporary Society* (New York: Doubleday, 1972). The concept of the wounded healer was developed by psychologist Carl Jung.

Pivot 5

FROM CONSUMING TO CREATING

Every time you spend money, you are casting your vote for the world you want.
—ANNA LAPPÉ

In the beginning God consumed. God said, "Let there be stuff to buy, television to watch, garbage to dump." God spent the evenings on the couch eating junk food and binge-watching movies. God consumed the earth's resources with no regard for the consequences for future generations. God worked nonstop to feed an endless need for more. Humankind was made in the image of God to be consumers.

Obviously, this is not what Scripture says about God. The Genesis account offers a much different picture! But if we are honest, the ways in which we live might communicate this about our God.

We know the nature of God is to create, and we know that we are made in God's image. Yet we spend so much of our lives centered on consuming rather than creating.

COUNTERING THE GOSPEL OF CONSUMERISM
From early on in life, we are taught to be consumers. Some estimates suggest that we are exposed to three thousand to five

thousand ads per day.[1] These messages try to convince us that our life's purpose is to consume. Corporations spend billions each year to turn us into consumers. We stand in long lines to be the first to buy the newest Apple product (Apple spent $933 million in advertising in 2011 alone to get us to do so).[2] We go faithfully to the movie theaters to sit passively, watching other people do things, go places, and experience life. We consume news and spend increased time scrolling on our favorite digital platforms. Social media is literally changing the way our brains work. We are being rewired (discipled?) into the gospel of consumerism. As parents, teachers, and mentors, we have to be careful that we are not inadvertently discipling the next generation to be consumers as well.

The gospel of consumerism has three core tenets: (1) we are created to be individual consumers; (2) we are meant to be passive; (3) our sole duty is to consume more.

The first tenet relates to our identity: who we are and how we see ourselves. The second tenet relates to our agency: how empowered we are to effect change and engage the world around us. The third tenet relates to our purpose: what is our reason for being and our way of life. The gospel of consumerism infiltrates every part of our personhood and runs counter to soul force and the God revealed in Scripture.

God is not a consumer. God is a creator. Being created in the image of God means we are made to create too. Ephesians 2:10 says that we are "created in Christ Jesus for good works, which God prepared beforehand to be our way of life." There are three

<hr>

1. Thirty years ago, a study by the Yankelovich Center for Social Science Research concluded that Americans saw two thousand ads per day; today it's estimated at five thousand. If you include every time you pass by a label in a grocery store, all the ads in your mailbox, the labels on everything you wear, the condiments in your fridge, the cars on the highway, it's closer to twenty thousand ads a day. See Sheree Johnson, "New Research Sheds Light on Daily Ad Exposures," SJ Insights, September 29, 2014, https://sjinsights.net/2014/09/29/new-research-sheds-light-on-daily-ad-exposures/.

2. "Who Spends More on Ads—Apple or Microsoft? Another Lesson in Quality Versus Quantity," Forbes, August 2, 2012, https://www.forbes.com/sites/ycharts/2012/08/02/who-spends-more-on-ads-apple-or-microsoft-another-lesson-in-quality-vs-quantity/#301221957e37.

powerful affirmations in this verse that counter the gospel of consumerism and remind us who we were really created to be.

We are meant to create, not consume

According to Ephesians 2, God is an artist and we are God's art. If God is an artist, then being creative and doing art is a spiritual practice! Every poem we write, song we sing, and piece of art we make is an affirmation of who God is and who we are created to be. We are created in the image of a creative God to be creative. Creativity is not reserved for making art; it is also necessary for thinking, loving, and living differently. Creativity is absolutely necessary for unleashing soul force.

In *An Other Kingdom: Departing the Consumer Culture*, John McKnight, Peter Block, and Walter Brueggemann offer an analysis of our current economy and its basis in consumption:

> If we want to follow the signs of the times, we have to look at how our core economic beliefs have produced a culture that makes poverty, violence, ill health, and fragile economic systems seem inevitable. Economic systems based on competition, scarcity, and acquisitiveness have become more than a question of economics; they have become the kingdom within which we dwell. That way of thinking invades our social order, our ways of being together, and what we value. It replicates the kingdom of ancient Egypt, Pharaoh's kingdom. It produces a consumer culture that centralizes wealth and power and leaves the rest wanting what the beneficiaries of the system have.[3]

Consumer culture did not happen by accident. Shortly after World War II, retail analyst Victor Lebow described the way Americans were trying to solve their economic challenges: "Our enormously productive economy demands that we make consumption our way of life, that we convert the buying and use of goods into rituals, that we seek our spiritual satisfaction, our ego

---

3. John McKnight, Peter Block, and Walter Brueggemann, *An Other Kingdom: Departing the Consumer Culture* (Hoboken: Wiley, 2016), xiii–xiv.

satisfaction, in consumption. . . . We need things consumed, burned up, replaced, and discarded at an ever increasing pace."[4]

The chair of President Eisenhower's council of economic advisors declared: "The American economy's ultimate purpose is to produce more consumer goods."[5] Perhaps this is why, after the 9/11 terrorist attack, President George W. Bush told the nation to go shopping. He could have urged the nation to create change, to build a culture of neighborliness, to inspire others, to fill the world with beauty rather than violence.

With the increase in multinational corporations and the interdependence of global markets, consumer culture is not restricted to America or even Western capitalist countries. Now that corporations constitute over half of the world's top one hundred economies—sixty-nine out of a hundred—the influence of consumer culture will only gain steam throughout the rest of the world.[6] Cultivating soul force can help us resist these globalizing forces.

We are created to be active, not passive

The Ephesians 2 passage says we are "created in Christ Jesus for good works." We were meant to be active, not passive. Our creativity and art should guide us to the good and spur us to be active agents of change in the world. Just as God brings light into the world through the spoken word, so do our words create something new in the world. We have the potential to shape culture, shift laws, and speak life through our creative actions.

The alternative to *consumer* culture, according to McKnight, Block, and Brueggemann, is a *covenantal* culture, one marked by creativity and community. "The alternative to the free market consumer culture is a set of covenants that supports neighborly disciplines, rather than market disciplines, as a producer of culture,"

---

4. Quoted (with slight variation) in David Suzuki, "Consumer Culture Is No Accident," Eartheasy, March 29, 2009, http://learn.eartheasy.com/2009/03/consumer-culture-is-no-accident/. The original appears in Victor Lebow, "Price Competition in 1955," *Journal of Retailing* 31, no. 1 (Spring 1955), 7.

5. Ibid.

6. Duncan Green, "The World's Top Economies: 31 Countries; 69 Corporations," World Bank, September 20, 2016, https://blogs.worldbank.org/publicsphere/world-s-top-100-economies-31-countries-69-corporations.

they write. "These non-market disciplines have to do with the common good and abundance as opposed to self-interest and scarcity."[7]

If we learned to consume, we can also learn to create and build community. We can discover and develop our creative voices. We need artists now more than ever to reimagine what the world can look like—a world of solidarity, mutual interest, compassion, and peace. The way things are now is not how they have to be. We are called to be creators, not consumers. We have the power to bring into reality a more beautiful, communal, and just world. We have the resource of soul force within us. We need not wait; we can begin now.

We are created on purpose, not by chance

Finally, Ephesians 2:10 states that we are "created in Christ Jesus for good works, which God prepared beforehand to be our way of life." We were intended to be artist-activists: creatives with a cause. Our creativity and gifts are given for the purpose of benefiting others. Our artistic inclinations are not accidents. Every breath and act is embedded with purpose. This doesn't mean every action of ours is scripted. It does mean that every action is significant, because we all are part of a larger story—the redemption of the world. And as co-creators with God, we get to write our story with God. When we allow ourselves to become passive consumers, we reflect an inaccurate picture of God and also miss out on the creative potential and purpose of our lives with God.

Isaiah Makar is a young man with vision and drive. You don't have to spend a lot of time around him to see that he is artistically gifted, funny, and serious about making an impact in the world. Isaiah shared his story with us. It's a story of pivoting from being a passive consumer of cultural stereotypes to becoming an active spoken word artist and business entrepreneur.

Life is funny. When I was a freshman at Oak Park and River Forest High School (OPRF) in 2005, prior to showing interest in spoken word, I fulfilled the partial image of a stereotypical

---

7. McKnight et al., *An Other Kingdom*, 6–7.

African American teenager. Clothes two sizes too big, LeBron
James jersey, Air Force Ones, sometimes afro, sometimes corn-
rows, and always the color-changing chain looped around my
neck with the Jesus piece medallion swaying to and fro to the
rhythm of my stroll. I wasn't a basketball player (I tried out
for the team, didn't make it), but eventually, I learned how to
dribble a ballpoint pen poetically on paper.

I remember laughing to myself. While walking home from
school, this guy says to me, "Hey man. You go to OPRF?" I tell
him yeah. He says, "I heard the spoken word club over there is
pretty good. Have you ever considered joining?" I reply with a
simple "Nope." Before he lets me leave, he makes his final pitch:
"Man, you should consider joining. It's a good way to get the
girls!"

I laughed. Not at the idea of joining the spoken word club to be
Mr. Casanova, but at the idea that I'd need to join the spoken
word club to "get" girls in the first place! (Yeah, I know, pretty
arrogant.) However, it wasn't until finally joining the spoken
word club my junior year that I realized I was the one who was
the joke.

"I wanna join the spoken word club," I said to the OPRF
Spoken Word director. His response? Let's just say there was
enough laughter in his office to mistake it for The Second City
comedy club. "Aren't you the same one who said one, you hate
poetry, and two, you never would join?"

I told him I had taught myself how to write poetry over the past
few years, and I wanted to give it a shot onstage. A few months
later, I performed for the first time, and before graduating in
2009, I had performed in four spoken word showcases!

Now I am teaching poetry to middle and high schoolers in my
hometown of Oak Park. And like a clever punch line, I never
saw this coming! The irony of being back in the classroom, this
time as the teacher, is the parallelism of the past and future. I
see a lot of students trying to be someone they are not based
on what they learn through media influences. This was me. The
hair, the clothes, the chain, and any other materialistic item I
decorated my lack of self-esteem with—these were displays of

me not knowing myself. Witnessing students being sucked into this has led to me redesigning my approach to teaching.

Allowing students to create their own experiences grants them permission to re-create themselves and their perceptions. It allows them to rely more on imagination. It allows them to tap into the art of resourcefulness: "artrepreneurship."

Whether it be in a classroom, on a sales floor, or in an emergency room, performance exists where there are people being served. Artrepreneurship is taking one's craft and rendering it into a business. Showing my students they can be performers anywhere opens their minds to the endless possibilities of what they can do with their poetry skills.

And to think I once laughed at the idea of spoken word! The best moments in life are the ones that strike you when you didn't see them coming—just like a punch line.

Notice that when Isaiah became less interested in materialistic things and more interested in making room for other students to be transformed by the spoken word, he became less of a consumer and more of a creator. Like Isaiah, we can leverage our own creativity when we focus less on acquiring things and more on generating change and beauty.

REIMAGINING THE WORLD: THE PIVOT TO CREATING

Consumerism is degenerative; creativity is generative. Many companies enlist a strategy of planned obsolescence. *The Economist* defines planned obsolescence as "a business strategy in which the obsolescence (the process of becoming obsolete—that is, unfashionable or no longer usable) of a product is planned and built into it from its inception. This is done so that in [the] future the consumer feels a need to purchase new products and services that the manufacturer brings out as replacements for the old ones."[8]

---

8. "Planned Obsolescence," *The Economist*, March 23, 2009, http://www.economist .com/node/13354332, adapted from Tim Hindle, *The Economist Guide to Management Ideas and Gurus* (London: Profile, 2008).

One alarming report states that 99 percent of the materials we harvest, mine, transport, process, and consume (including the goods themselves) are trash within six months.[9] Consumption supports a cycle of deterioration and waste that is not sustainable for the planet. In contrast, creativity is life giving and life sustaining. Creativity breeds creativity.

Consuming less creates more beauty

Kate Pollard, a mother of two and an aspiring writer, has spent the last few years wrestling with what it means to resist the cycles of consumption by spending less and creating more room for beauty. Here's what she told us:

One of my core guiding values is to practice thoughtfulness when it comes to what I invest in. Who makes the things we consume? What are their working conditions, and do they receive a fair wage for the product they created? How am I reducing unnecessary waste? Is there an option to fill this need more creatively with something we already own and can repurpose? Does this purchase fulfill a true need, or is it simply a want? Do my neighbors have access to this good as well—and if they don't, what does it mean for me to leverage my privilege accordingly? Am I buying locally whenever possible so that I'm continually contributing to my community's voice and ability to hold space for the good of many rather than the profit of a few?

We do a lot of research before making most purchases. While this does mean everything tends to take a little longer and cost a little more, things then need to be replaced less frequently and help us stay true to our commitment of valuing people and experiences over possessions. I have a list of places I already know and trust as providing ethically sourced products, as well as a list of places I simply don't frequent. We love thrift stores, yard sales, Craigslist, and hand-me-downs. Whenever possible,

---

9. Annie Leonard, "*The Story of Stuff*: Referenced and Annotated Script," The Story of Stuff (website), accessed January 20, 2018, https://storyofstuff.org/wp-content/uploads/movies/scripts/Story%20of%20Stuff.pdf. This percentage refers not just to the goods or products themselves, but to all the materials used to produce, package, and ship those items.

we choose to invest in the talent and handiwork of our friends, which means many of our things are as beautiful as they are functional.

Don't get me wrong; I'm not perfect. I still have a long way to go in my pursuit of both minimalism and generosity—after all, aren't these two sides of the same coin? But I love that asking all of these questions has led to simple, habitual rhythms of life for our family. I love that I can look around our house and have a meaningful story to share about nearly everything we own. And I love that this is one small, sustainable way I have of navigating my own privilege. It also helps me continue to stay in the tension of discerning what form solidarity will take with my neighbors who don't have the same choice.

The freedom of simplicity

In *The Freedom of Simplicity*, Richard Foster argues that simplicity is good for our souls because it "frees us from this modern mania" that "more is better."[10] I (Shawn) truly desire this freedom, and on occasion have even caught glimpses of it as I have sought to embrace a lifestyle of simplicity. Unfortunately, many times I have experienced simplicity as something more like a straitjacket that restricts my freedom and holds me hostage to guilt for having more stuff than I need.

Indeed, it is possible to feel the burden of simplicity like a weight around our necks. For many of us, simplicity is something that condemns rather than liberates us. We feel the call to live simply as an incessant demand—a constant reminder of our not-good-enough-ness—rather than a grace-filled invitation to see that what we are and what we have is already enough! Simplicity becomes another way we try to earn God's love or prove our worth.

Worse, it can become another attempt to show we're better than those who don't live as simply or who aren't as socially conscious as we are. I call this being a "justice Pharisee." In many social justice circles, simplicity can begin to seem like a competition about

---

10. Richard J. Foster, *The Freedom of Simplicity: Finding Harmony in a Complex World* (San Francisco: Harper, 1989), 3.

who can live more simply. It's like a high school pep rally: "We live simply, yes we do! We live simply, how 'bout *you?*"

I know this because I have struggled with this for many years. Sometimes, no matter how many bags of giveaways I dropped off at my local thrift store or homeless shelter, I never felt that I was living simply enough. I suffered from what you might call "simplicity bulimia": a compulsive urge to purge all one's belongings to feel better about oneself. Much like someone wrestling with unrealistic body image, I had unrealistic standards of what "the simple way" was supposed to look like! Is it better to buy sweatshop-free clothing? Is it better to get your clothes from a thrift store? Is it better to make your own clothes? Is it better to not wear clothes at all?

After a lot of internal turmoil, I realized that the unattainable standard of simplicity I was holding on to was counter to the freedom of simplicity toward which God was calling me. Since then I have learned a few things that have helped me move away from a guilt-ridden, restrictive, legalistic approach and toward a gentle, grace-filled, and generous simplicity.

There is not one standard of simplicity for everyone. Be your own gauge and standard for acceptable simplicity. Make these decisions according to your unique calling and what you sense soul force leading you to.

Be led by the Spirit rather than by "shoulds." Take the counsel of Jesuit writer James Martin and stop "shoulding all over yourself."[11] Instead of feeling perpetually guilty, seek what the Spirit of grace and freedom is leading you toward. What feels most freeing, rather than most obligatory? Seeing simplicity as a choice helps us be free to be led by the Spirit.

Create your own set of guiding principles. Everything my wife and I have aligns with one of these three guiding principles. Each possession is (1) a necessity, (2) something we are willing to share, or (3) something that inspires beauty. We are slowly but surely learning the freedom of simplicity. Simplicity is not a hard-and-fast rule to bind us to an impossible standard, but a Spirit-led,

11. James Martin, SJ, *The Jesuit Guide to (Almost) Everything: A Spirituality for Real Life* (New York: HarperOne, 2010), 329.

personal journey to discover grace and freedom in all things, even our stuff.

The privilege of simplicity; the promise of sustainability

Being able to choose simplicity is itself a privilege, for privilege is having the freedom to choose. The more choices we have, the more privilege we hold. For people coming from places of relative privilege, simplicity often takes the form of downward mobility and living a more minimalist lifestyle. But people living in poverty or lacking material resources are already living a forced simplicity. They may actually need to be on an upward trajectory in order to be healthy and whole.

Thus, insisting on a standard of simplicity for people who have already experienced poverty or oppression could actually be harmful. This point was driven home for us when one of our friends went to a Christian music festival that was focused on social justice. Justice and simplicity were core values of the festival, so there were justice-themed workshops, exhibit booths, and even a sample "tiny home" for participants to explore. Tiny homes have become popular among a growing number of millennials and socially minded people who are attracted to a downwardly mobile lifestyle. When our friend was asked if she was interested in viewing the home, she gasped and said, "I spent nine years in prison. I never want to live in a box again!" For someone who has grown up in spacious homes and felt the anxious pressure of the consumer cycle, the choice of a tiny home might bring a welcome freedom. But for someone who has been confined to a small bed in a dark cell for many years, a tiny home might feel more like a prison.

Consumption is not the answer to poverty, of course. For those who have lacked resources, part of the danger of materialism is that it locates worth outside of themselves. While both rich and poor believe the lie of consumption that tells us our worth is in what we have, those who have felt the stigma and degradation of poverty can be particularly vulnerable to the promises of status and worth that advertising offers. Instead of judging people in poverty for doing the same thing that many of us do, maybe we can extend compassion and understanding and work harder to remove the logs from our own consumerist eyes. Instead of blaming one another for falling prey to the allure of consumption, perhaps we can work together to resist the forces of consumerism and create a more sustainable system.

Sustainability may hold more promise for our world than the concept of simplicity. After all, the reason simplicity is needed is because the earth cannot sustain consumerist lifestyles. Sustainability reminds us that we live on a planet with limited resources and that our actions, however small, can have large-scale effects on other people across the world. Simplicity can be self-serving and keep us focused on "me." Sustainability, on the other hand, helps us remember we belong to a global family. When the world's richest 20 percent consumes almost 80 percent of the world's resources, then individual frugality will not be enough.[12] (If you live in a Western country, this probably applies to you.) To become sustainable, we will need a radical reordering of the entire consumer system. This is a collective effort that will take the courage and conviction of soul force over a lifetime, not simply when it's trending.

A call to come alive

The pivot to creativity is not only a call *away* from consumerism; it is also a call to come alive. "Don't ask what the world needs," Howard Thurman once said. "Ask what makes you come alive, and go do that, because what the world needs is people who have come alive."[13] Consumer culture ropes us into a lifestyle of overconsumption and debt that makes it harder for us to pursue what makes us come alive. We are constantly trying to keep up with car loans, mortgages, student loans, and credit card debt. This is not the abundant life we were meant to live. A pivot away

---

12. The world's richest 20 percent consumes 76.6 percent of the world's resources; the middle 60 percent consumes 21.9 percent; and the poorest 20 percent consumes 1.5 percent. This is based on data of the share of private consumption in 2005 from the World Bank Indicators, 2008, as cited by Anup Shah, "Consumption and Consumerism," Global Issues, last modified January 5, 2014, http://www.globalissues.org/issue/235/consumption-and-consumerism.

13. Quoted in Gil Bailie, *Violence Unveiled: Humanity at the Crossroads* (New York: Crossroad Publishing, 1995), xv.

from consuming and toward creating involves an awareness of and awakening to what makes us come alive.

Some of us are literally killing ourselves trying to keep up in a career when we could be coming alive in our calling. Our friend Fajr Allen was working hard to pursue the American dream. But the energy needed to maintain a consumer lifestyle, coupled with the stress of being in a job that did not bring life, began to affect her health. She suffered from a variety of gastrointestinal issues, an aggressive case of alopecia areata (extreme hair loss), brain fog, chronic fatigue, muscle spasms, severe joint pain, and migraine headaches. Despite this debilitating reality, doctors told her that she was a pillar of health.

So at the age of forty-three, Allen decided to become a stay-at-home wife and mother, and she spent more than two years searching for remedies. Every doctor she saw responded with an ineffective prescription and a pat on the back, sending her on her way. She figured her health issues were related to age and motherhood, but after meeting with a personal trainer, she realized her medical issues were a direct result of unmanaged stress and poor eating habits. She had literally and figuratively been consuming the wrong things. She removed a variety of prepackaged and processed foods from her diet and replaced them with whole, organic foods. That, along with yoga and semi-regular exercise, made her feel as if she had shed her old body and put on a new one—hair included.

This realization led to a deeper and more intense desire to gain knowledge that would lead to the improved health of her entire family. She has since become her family's resident nutritionist and health coach. She even helped nurse her mother-in-law back to health after she suffered a mild stroke. It is her hope to continue to share her journey with those who feel that wellness is out of their reach.

Allen has found the courage to take her passions beyond her kitchen table and has even forged a partnership with Communities First Association and L!VE Café. L!VE Café now sells Allen's gluten-free, organic foods to its customers, allowing her yet another avenue to share her passions for cooking and wellness. She is now planning to launch her own website to share her journey, offer coaching, and encourage others to rethink the American diet and lifestyle.

A pivot from consuming to creating has helped Allen come alive in her calling and helped others come alive too. This is the beauty of soul force. It not only ignites a fire within our hearts, but becomes contagious, igniting a spark in others around us. Our hope is that every reader catches this fire. Life is too short to neglect the gifts and passions inside us. We are more than consumers; we each have a calling to come alive that is just waiting to be discovered.

SOUL FORCE STORY

From consuming to creating

Lanecia Rouse Tinsley

As a Houstonian professional and creative artist, I make art, create space, and tap into partnerships with other creatives and activists toward community development and justice.

Raised in South Carolina, I am one of two daughters of an artist mother and a father who is a United Methodist pastor. They encouraged us to follow our dreams and use our gifts to make the world a better place. It was a great home in which to grow up. It was also hard growing up, however, because my father was specifically called to ministry in the area of racial reconciliation; he was the first Black pastor to be placed at a large white Methodist church in the 1980s. At a young age, I saw the power of racism to destroy community relationships, foster injustice, and keep people apart.

It was good to watch my father move around the city, inside and outside the church, bringing people together. He would face the most disgusting, hurtful things with strength, kindness, and love. He wasn't afraid to speak up.

I grew up suppressing a lot of emotion, because I wanted to fit in. I went to a white church and lived in a white neighborhood. I wasn't Black enough for the Black kids, and I was too Black for the white kids. It caused a lot of identity questions and internal wrestling that lasted until I went to Duke Divinity School.

There I took a course called The Fallacy of Race. I remember crying in my professor's office and sharing my story. He said, "You have lived a biracial existence in a Black body." He encouraged me to sit with that reality, and to begin to have conversations with and listen to people who grew up biracial and had to navigate this "both/and" versus "either/or" world. That helped me begin to embrace my identity and own my Blackness.

After taking a couple of pastoral appointments, I became restless and started struggling with depression. I had a general sense I wasn't where I belonged. I crossed paths with Rudy and Juanita Rasmus, copastors of St. John's United Methodist Church in downtown Houston. St. John's is an incredibly diverse congregation of almost ten thousand people, a full third of whom have been homeless at one point or another. Rudy and Juanita also cofounded Bread of Life, a nonprofit that has been caring for the homeless for two decades.

One day Rudy asked me, "How long are you able to continue this path? Until you are dead inside?" I hadn't met this man before, but he spoke to what I was internally asking myself but had been afraid to answer.

Later, I experienced a depressive breaking point that required a clinician. I called Rudy and told him I had to choose life, and I needed to go some place for mental health care. His response: "Why don't you come to Houston, and let us love on you?" That sounded a lot better than going to some clinic. I hung out in Houston and allowed people to love me. I got to meet people who had gone through depression and breakdowns, and they loved me to a place of healing.

I saw the work they were doing among men and women living outdoors. This was the kind of work I wanted to be part of. Juanita shared her dream to start an art project among the men and women who took part in Bread of Life, and eventually I received an invitation to come. The Art Project was a perfect fusion of passions and curiosities and longings I had. In 2011, I relocated to Houston to get The Art Project off the ground. The vision was to create space for men and women living on the streets or transitioning out of homelessness to have a therapeutic experience through the arts, for mental, emotional, and spiritual healing. Not everyone who came through The Art Project was the next Picasso, but they were all given the opportunity to encounter beauty and to create. We all long to add something to the world.

The Art Project still does amazing work. It provided me time and space to explore my passion for the arts. Setting up workshops for participants, I started creating alongside them. Then participants in the project taught me their techniques. I realized my own artistic gifts.

Seeking to thrive created this courage within me to speak boldly. I started saying, "I want to be a professional artist. What does that take? I should get a studio downtown. What does that take?" I got a studio before I left my full-time job. I started creating. All I wanted to do was be in the studio. I started saving up money, writing up a small business plan, and finally decided it was time to move on from my job and pursue art full-time.

The concepts I deal with in my art are joy and sorrow and the complexities and beauties of life. My eyes are searching for beauty in unexpected places. I photograph some of the most ordinary things, things that others may have missed. When I was in my deepest moments of depression and deep grief, beauty and creativity were essential to my making it through. In the same way we hunger and thirst for bread, we have a need for beauty and creativity. I want to create beauty, art, and space for people to create. The work I do in racial justice and solidarity is about imagination. It's going to take creativity and imagination for us to reconstruct new ways of being.

SOUL FORCE PIVOT POINTS

Create
What are ways you are feeling drawn to be creative? Are you consuming more than you are creating? Where can you make more space for creativity?

Live simply
What can be freeing about simplicity? What do your spending patterns communicate about your values? What is the invitation for you in simplicity?

Create your own guiding principles
Do you tend to get legalistic about your convictions? How can you develop balance? How are your commitments building community? What guiding principles do you have or need around consumption?

Seek sustainability
Move beyond simplicity to sustainability. Seek to understand the connections between those who have excess and those who don't have enough. How can you use your creativity to address sustainability? What systems need to be reimagined to be more equitable?

Pursue your passion
Are you doing what you love? What makes you come alive? What have you been dreaming about doing but haven't acted on, perhaps because of fear, a mentality of scarcity, or a lack of time? What small step can you take now toward your dream?

PIVOT 5 MANTRA

I am created to create.

Pivot 6

FROM CHARITY
TO CHANGE

While we do our good works let us not forget that the real solution lies in a world in which charity will have become unnecessary.
—CHINUA ACHEBE, *ANTHILLS OF THE SAVANNAH*

If gun violence plagued your city and you wanted to bring about change, how would you go about it? Would you mentor youth one-on-one to keep them off the streets or write a check for support services to individuals affected by violence? Would you listen to community needs and support community solutions emerging from local leaders? Would you seek to change gun laws or direct more funding to the most underfunded communities across the city?

Your response to a challenge will largely depend on what you believe about change. This chapter looks at how change happens and how we can pivot from a one-dimensional charity approach to a robust and holistic model of transformative change.

THREE THEORIES OF CHANGE

Everyone has a theory for change. Most theories of change can be summarized into three major categories.

Theory 1

Some believe that individuals change the world. The Russian novelist and historian Aleksandr Solzhenitsyn believed if we want to change the world, we should begin with ourselves. "I believe if we begin with ourselves and do the things that we need to do and become the best person we can be, we have a much better chance of changing the world for the better." This is the *individualist* mindset. Individualists believe that you change the world one relationship, one student, one cup of coffee at a time. This centers power and responsibility on the individual. This theory gives individuals hope that one person can indeed change the world.

Theory 2

Some believe that communities change the world. This is reminiscent of the famous quote, widely attributed to Margaret Mead, that says, "Never doubt that a small group of thoughtful, committed citizens can change the world. It is the only thing that ever has." This is the *collectivist* mindset. Those who hold to this theory believe in the power of the people, the collective, to change the world. While the individualist believes in the power of *one*, the collectivist believes in the power of *everyone*. Collectivists, for example, spend their time forming intentional communities, nurturing capacity through asset-based community development, and implementing community organizing strategies.

Theory 3

Still others believe that changing systems changes the world. This is reflected in George Orwell's notion that "one's got to change the system, or one changes nothing."[1] This is the *activist*, or reformer, mindset. The activist understands the ways the environment and systems affect individuals and communities. Activists often engage in advocacy and activism to bring about changes to policies and systems.

---

1. George Orwell, *Keep the Aspidistra Flying* (New York: Harcourt, 1969), 164. First published 1936.

6.1 Strengths and dangers of each change model

Change model	Strengths	Dangers	Change methods
Individualist-personal	1. Belief in the power one person can wield 2. An emphasis on the importance of relationships 3. Stresses personal accountability	1. Often ends in a charity mindset 2. Fails to examine systems and their impact 3. Lacks understanding of root causes	Individual charity; one-to-one relationships; coaching; counseling; self-help
Collectivist-communal	1. Believes in the power of communities 2. Highlights assets and strengths of community 3. Creates web of solidarity between diverse people	1. Undermines personal responsibility 2. Fails to see systemic impact on communities 3. Addresses symptoms, not root causes	Asset-based community development; community organizing; relief and development; intentional communities
Activist-systemic	1. Allows understanding of larger forces at work (political, economic, generational, global) 2. Addresses root causes 3. Has potential for wide-ranging effect	1. Underplays individual agency and accountability 2. Fails to see impact of relationships and community 3. Can become removed from people and communities	Advocacy; public policy; voting; nonviolent protest

But which theory is correct? Doesn't each one ring true in some way?

We believe that change happens via all three. Change is a dynamic interplay between individuals, communities, *and* systems.

DYNAMIC AND INTERSECTIONAL CHANGE

Soul force takes us beyond individual charity acts to deep, meaningful change in personal relationships, community development, and systemic change. As you can hopefully tell by now, this book follows this framework. Soul force starts with the personal and emanates outward to solidarity in community and then to

6.2 Integrated change models

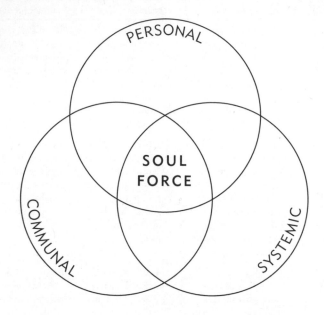

systemic change and societal impact. If *Soul Force* stopped at the individual level, this book would only be a self-help book. If this book stopped at the community level, it would be another community development or community organizing manual. If we only addressed systemic factors in these pages, then this book would deny the personal and communal nature of our humanity. But as we connect the personal, the communal, and the systemic, soul force is activated to create intersectional change. Let's look at each of these types of change in a bit more depth.

The personal is often the entry point, but it cannot be the endpoint. An intersectional approach acknowledges how the personal, communal, and systemic shape and inform one another. While Gandhi encouraged individuals to be the change they wanted to see in the world, he also knew that if alternative communities weren't created and institutions and policies weren't reformed, then the change would fall short. Likewise, while Martin Luther King focused on changing discriminatory federal policies around issues like housing segregation, military spending, and class equity, he never lost sight of the community he was seeking to create. For King, the end goal was not changed individuals or changed social policies, although they were both important. The end goal was the beloved community. When we focus on only one change model, we risk leaving out important factors and limiting our impact for change.

CORE PRINCIPLES OF PERSONAL CHANGE

We have already shared quite a bit about the importance of personal change and the necessity of examining our own fears, internal barriers, and soul care practices, especially when doing justice work. In chapter 3, we talked about moving from selfishness to solidarity and how living with people who are not like us actually expands our worldview and enhances our lived experience. In chapter 4, we took a hard look at the significance of what it means to turn from hurt to hope, which is often a personal effort. The core principles of personal change have been discussed at length in previous chapters, because the movement of soul force goes from the inside out. We recognize the importance of searching our own hearts and minds before engaging in community with others and seeking to foster systemic change, so we won't spend as much time here on this level of change.

We do want to touch on the unique strengths and dangers of the personal level. Its strengths are the belief in the power of one to make a difference. Some of our favorite Scripture stories, Hollywood movies, and community heroes attest to the truth that one person can truly make a difference in the world. Amid towering injustice and crippling forces of evil, it is reassuring to know that we can at least change the world by changing ourselves. We can also influence the life of another human being. The personal approach deeply values personal relationships and stresses personal responsibility. In life, we may not be able to control everything around us, but we can do the things that are in our power to do. Often, this is all we need to do to make a world of difference in our lives and in the lives of others. This is the power of the personal approach.

The danger of the personal approach, however, is that we can come to rely on an individual charity approach to solve community and structural issues. The personal approach can leave unfair systems unexamined and fail to register the impact of communal and structural barriers. When we only see individually, we often assign individual causes to social inequalities. In *Divided by Faith*, authors Christian Smith and Michael Emerson show how conservative evangelicals have a hard time seeing systems and are particularly prone to blaming economic disparities of race and class on individual shortcomings rather than structural injustice.[2] The personal approach is a powerful means of bringing about change, but it is limited by itself.

So let's take a look at some of the core principles of communal and systemic change.

CORE PRINCIPLES OF COMMUNAL CHANGE

Soul force takes us beyond charity work and personal change to engage in community building so that we can bring about collective change. I (Reesheda) train leaders, churches, and organizations in asset-based community development—also known as ABCD—so they can maximize their impact for change in the places where they are. ABCD is an approach to community organizing and development that starts with the strengths and capacities present within the community rather than beginning with its deficits. Ministers, social workers, organizers, and other helping professionals often start their work by asking, "What does this community need? What are the problems we need to solve?" The story then becomes one of deficiency, crisis, toxicity, and helplessness.

ABCD starts from a very different place. It begins by asking, "What assets does this community hold? What makes this community unique and strong, and how can those strengths be extended and multiplied?"

The problem with problem-solving

The first thing we often do when we go into a new community is analyze it. In a consumerist and capitalist society, it is almost

---

2. Michael Emerson and Christian Smith, *Divided by Faith: Evangelical Religion and the Problem of Race in America* (Oxford: Oxford University Press, 2000).

second nature for us to find out what's wrong. Solutions are profitable. From kindergarten through graduate school, we have learned that identifying what's wrong and creating a solution is profitable. When you are given a problem in math or science or English, you solve the problem and then you get something. Before there is money involved, you get a grade. You are taught to work for a higher grade—the more valuable one. You go through your whole academic career learning to look for what's wrong, find the answer, and then wait for your ROI (return on investment). You invested your time and your thinking and your ability to solve a problem. What are you going to get back? It's transactional. In almost everything we do, this is the model.

So it makes perfect sense that we would go into a neighborhood, a work environment, an institution, or a relationship and ask, "What am I going to help them see that's wrong? How am I going to identify their deficit or challenge and respond to it in a way that maximizes the return?" Our whole lives we have been trained to think in terms of finding solutions. So finding solutions in a neighborhood might look like identifying that it's crime ridden, or noticing that there's illiteracy, or noticing that it's not well kept, or that there's generational decay. When we do that, it becomes second nature to say what we think the solution should be.

When I (Reesheda) was in Congo with a team of people a few years ago, one person in my group noticed there were lots of children. "Why are there all these kids everywhere?" this person said. "All they do is make babies over here. Maybe they could solve their poverty issues if they could just stop having babies."

My thought was this: I don't know why there are so many kids here, but I'm willing to bet if the solution were that simple, the people would have already come up with it themselves. There may be some underlying issues—or maybe there aren't even any "issues" at all! Maybe people in this community find joy in having lots of babies. Maybe they see children as gifts, and as gifts that offer hope in the middle of challenges of daily life. And maybe they will find a way to solve their problems that has nothing to do with diminishing the number of babies they have in their community.

If you can think of the solution for a community within minutes of stepping foot on its soil—well, it's probably not an actual
solution. Also, someone else has probably already thought of it!
If you catch yourself doing this, check your impulse. If you don't
have the lens, run it by someone who does. How awesome does it
feel to come into a community and solve its problems in the first
five minutes you've been there? That's not genius status. That's
paternalism. People have been struggling for four hundred years,
and then we show up and the problem is solved? We must learn
to see the paternalism implicit in that posture. We are implying
that we must be smarter, more thoughtful, and more intuitive than
every single person in the entire place if we can solve their problems in a matter of minutes. It's laughable, but we do it anyway.

This doesn't mean that we don't have gifts to share with others.
It just means there's a posture that comes with that sharing—a
posture that acknowledges gifts and strengths and talents over
deficits and challenges. Otherwise, we end up with a shallow type
of charity or a paternalistic form of development. Paternalism tries
to fix something that the rest of the community may not even see
as broken.

The core principles of ABCD are as follows:

- Listen to the community to acquire history, context, story,
  and values.
- Listen to the community to determine what the felt and
  expressed needs of the community are.
- Mine the community *with* the community to capture the
  myriad of assets present there.
- Work *with* the community to devise strategies led by the
  community to mobilize the assets within that community
  toward the expressed felt needs of that community.
- Leverage one's access to organizational and institutional
  power and wealth in concert with the movement already
  established and led by indigenous leaders of the community.
- Reveal and coach indigenous leaders to continue the movement as you (the person of power and influence) plan
  your succession.

ABCD is a lifestyle

Asset-based community development is more than what you do; it's a lifestyle you choose. ABCD changes your mindset and perspective—the way you see people and the world. It is not something to be applied to just your work, or ministry, or business. ABCD is a lifestyle that permeates all of your life. We are more than writers describing concepts; this is part of our lived experience. In between writing, both of us are on the ground in our communities, connecting with people, asking questions, pausing to reflect on not only what we are doing but how we are doing it. ABCD is something we strive to live and breathe in big and small ways throughout our personal and professional lives.

Essentially, ABCD is a way of life in which you work every day to see the gifts, strengths, talents, and assets of others, yourself, and your environment. This is not to say that you ignore the challenges and deficits that exist, but that you have a commitment to maximizing the gifts and talents that are present. What is nonnegotiable, however, is that there are always gifts, strengths, talents, and assets present.

If you go somewhere or are with someone or a group and you cannot see the assets in that space, in that person, or in that group of people, you need to look harder. Sometimes our lenses are blurred. Sometimes seeing these strengths will require intentional help and support from the people who have a better lens for the context than you do. Asking for that help and support is important and vital.

If you are in a place or with a person or group in which you cannot identify assets, then your choice is to either (a) continue *not* to see them on your own, or (b) find someone who has eyes to see and ears to hear those assets better than you can. We challenge you to choose the latter. Every time. Do it unapologetically, and do it relentlessly. Do it afraid. Do it humbly. Do it foolishly. When you build relationships in a community from a starting point of seeing the deficits, you don't get to see the beauty, the gifts, and the image of God in that place or in those people.

If elements of your personhood have traditionally been marginalized, look inside yourself. If even part of your identity has been historically marginalized, and if the messaging you have received has been denigrating, subjugating, paternalistic, and colonizing, start by examining the gifts, strengths, and talents of that part of yourself. As a Black woman who grew up in a place sometimes called "poor" but that I would call "intentionally disadvantaged," I (Reesheda) would then have to do a reexamination of what it means to be Black, female, and intentionally disadvantaged in America. What are the gifts and strengths associated with "womanness"? What are the gifts and strengths and talents of my Blackness? What are the gifts and strengths of the community from which I have come?

As I ask these questions, I begin to redesign and redefine a new set of gifts, strengths, and talents. Not that those strengths weren't there before; I'm simply redefining them in a way that is counter to how they have been traditionally defined *for me* in the past. What does it mean to be a Black woman from a neighborhood that has been socioeconomically disadvantaged intentionally? How do I redefine the way I see myself apart from the way the dominant culture has intended for me to see myself? Can I see the gifts, the strengths, the talents? In essence, do I see the *imago Dei*, "the face of God," in my Blackness, in my womanness, and in my neighborhood? This is how the personal work that we must do intersects with the communal and systemic work that we are committed to. Once we are able to find those gifts, strengths, and talents in ourselves, then we are ready to look for those gifts, strengths, and talents in other people and places.

Stop turning off the dark

Now imagine your community. Imagine the people, relationships, and institutions within it. Imagine their talents, strengths, and skills. Imagine that community living in shalom, the Hebrew word for the highest peace to which we can aspire.

Now think of the ways in which your community has not yet actualized shalom. What are the things that keep people from experiencing the fullness of shalom? We may think of violence, lack of resources, fear, systemic injustice. Some of these things might be the root cause, and some may be symptoms or outcomes. Why does it make a difference if we name causes or outcomes?

Jonathan Brooks, a colleague of ours and a community development–minded pastor on the South Side of Chicago, says he no longer uses the phrase "Stop the Violence." Rather than talking about stopping the violence, he talks about making peace happen. Brooks uses the metaphor of a dark room to symbolize violence. You don't go into a dark room and ask someone to "turn off the dark." That is a ridiculous concept. You *turn on the light.*

Similarly, you don't turn off the violence. You don't stop the violence. You increase the efforts of peace. "Turning off the dark" is outcome-based thinking. Outcome-based approaches attempt to engineer an outcome without getting to the heart of the cause. "Turning on the light," on the other hand, addresses root causes. When you address root causes, you diminish the thing that's creating the symptoms. That's what makes our work hard and slow, but it's also what makes our work resilient and sustainable when it's done well.

In Colossians 1:19-20, the apostle Paul writes that "for in him all the fullness of God was pleased to dwell, and through him God was pleased to reconcile to himself all things, whether on earth or in heaven, by making peace through the blood of his cross." Peace is made when light shines. Turning on the light is more resilient and sustainable than turning off the dark. It is with God and from God that peace and light emerge.

Learn to see what is around you

An experience from my (Reesheda's) time in Congo illustrates an important aspect of ABCD: learning to truly see what is happening in a community. Our group was traveling down a Congolese road one day when I exclaimed, "It's so refreshing to be here, because I am seeing so many things that Black folks do in our communities in the United States. I never knew the origin of some of those customs, but now I have a context for understanding that people in our communities have been doing these things for a long time."

My boss at the time, a white man, asked me, "Like what things?"

"Like everyone braids hair on porches here," I said. "At home, I like that we hang out on the porch and braid each other's hair. I like the way that it gets us outside so that we can visit with neighbors and build community and family. But I've wondered why people in other communities don't really do that. Now that I'm in Congo, it seems like every single porch we pass has someone on it, braiding hair. So now I understand that this is a practice that people brought with them when they were captured and enslaved. Now I get it."

There was a pause. Then my boss said, "People braid hair on the porch in Congo?"

"You've been here seventeen times!" I said.

"Yes, but I've never seen anyone braid hair on their porch," he replied.

I pointed out the window of our vehicle. "Look. Right there, and there. And there. How could you not see that?"

There was another silence. "I literally never saw that," he said. "Not even once."

Sometimes, given our perspective or what we are expecting to see, we do not see things that are right in front of our eyes. My boss's eyes literally did not register this practice—braiding hair on porches—that was happening all around him. I suspect that might have been because he was looking at other things: how many wells were there, because we needed to dig wells; or how many schools were there, because we needed to build schools.

When we adjust what we are looking for, it will absolutely determine what we see. When we commit to seeing the strength and beauty and capacity around us, we will see other things, such as a community's challenges, in light of the good.

CORE PRINCIPLES OF SYSTEMIC CHANGE

To pivot from charity to change, it will take going beyond individual charity and even beyond community development. We will need to nurture systemic change. When the dots are connected between the symptoms and the causes, and when we address structural issues, individuals, churches, and nonprofits will see greater changes happen.

Coté Soerens, founding executive director of Puentes Advocacy, Counseling, and Education, shared with us how incorporating a systemic mindset helped her organization pivot toward sustainable change.

I live in South Park, which I have come to call Seattle's best-kept secret. South Park is the most materially impoverished neighborhood in Seattle. Surrounded by industrial land, it doesn't make it into the hipster posters honoring the neighborhoods in our city. If you have heard of it, you may know it as a food desert, ridden with gangs and violent crime, or a great place to flip houses.

Yes, South Park has experienced chronic divestment. We have two highways cutting through our neighborhood, public transportation is so unpredictable that you can count on running to catch the bus as a part of your daily exercise, and a few years ago the neighborhood had to fight for the city to reopen the bridge that connects us to the rest of Seattle because the city closed it without a solution. We are a neighborhood of immigrants; 40 percent Latino, 20 percent Asian, and mostly working class. We are a living grant proposal. At least, that is one story we can tell about South Park.

But if you ask the people who live here, you will hear a different story: You will hear stories of solidarity, of community, and of "¡Sí, se puede!" (Yes, we can!). While we have many challenges, people are friendly and incredibly generous. Yet in a way, as a neighborhood, we are constantly caught in the tension between charity and grassroots change. And today, that tension is palpable, as we are faced with imminent displacement.

As Seattle struggles with rising housing prices and heightened population growth, our neighborhood is wrestling with the question of how to protect communities of color in South Park. That is why two years ago, I invited a group of Latina immigrant neighbors to a discernment retreat: to determine the change we wanted to see in our community. Housing justice for immigrants in South Park was a priority to our group, so we decided to organize.

We started meeting and applied for a grant from the Social Justice Fund to support our organizing. We started learning the complicated language of urban development and zoning, looking into innovative impact investment models to fund collective ownership of buildings and affordable housing. All of these learning conversations happened over homecooked meals, with children running around our table.

As our group has grown stronger in friendship and sisterhood, we have been able to lead our neighborhood at large into a generative conversation on housing justice. We have facilitated conversations with experts and advocates, built alliances to provide "Know Your Rights" workshops for tenants who are also immigrants, and implemented a neighborhood-wide asset-based community development initiative called Abundant Community.

Our group, which we have called Nuestro Barrio (Our Neighborhood), keeps growing in leadership based on the knowledge that everyone, no matter our immigration status, level of education, or income level, has something to give.

Soerens has continued her efforts in the development of sustainable change by equipping local leaders to lead Puentes. She has passed on the leadership of the organization she founded to talented leaders who also represent the community in which they serve. This is a telltale distinction of one who is moving from charity to change: a leader who literally works herself out of a job, having equipped others to take her place in effective, sustainable leadership.

Equity matters

The pivot to change is a pivot toward equity. It is not enough to talk about race, justice, and politics; we have to also talk about equity. To be clear, we are not just talking about everyone starting from the same starting point (equality). Rather, we are talking about everyone starting from the point that most ensures one's flourishing, given one's own current context and conditions (equity). Reconciliation and diversity do not go far enough. Representation is one facet, but equity is another. Looking at our churches, organizations, and communities through an equity lens brings about a deeper level of change.

We spoke with Anna Golladay, executive producer of the Inhabit Conference, who contends that the significant lack of equity in neighborhoods of color results in a lack of entrepreneurial opportunity and start-up support for small businesses. Despite the fact that many of these communities have been doing entrepreneurship well for generations, a lack of income equality is what keeps entrepreneurs in these communities from the level of success that they are otherwise poised to achieve.

For example, 70 percent of entrepreneurs rely on personal savings or family members for funding. Golladay pointed out that significant disparities in household wealth mean that, for people of color, there is not a high likelihood that "a rich uncle will appear with a check for new business start-up."

As a means to address this disparity, Golladay is encouraging churches to consider the following questions pertaining to their communities: What good is being done? Who is being served? What hope-filled message is being breathed into the lungs of the neighborhood? Golladay asserted that "the modern church would be more about her people than about her building," noting that "this type of evangelical work rarely happens singularly within the walls of a brick-and-mortar space."

Creating equity between faith communities would be one way to parlay space into action, Golladay said.

> Congregations should explore the biblical touchpoints of money and what it means to be a people who gift, not rent, their monetary and physical assets in ways that then flow back into the neighborhood in order to create economies of scale with others. What it might look like to reimagine a Sunday school room into a coworking space for folks that can't afford high speed Internet? What it might look like to convert unused space into a multistation area where some entrepre-

neurs make jewelry to sell on Etsy and others operate a seamstress or tailor business? Can churches open their commercial kitchens to food truck start-ups or neighborhood bakers who are baking pies to sell weekly at the farmers' market? What it would look like to offer a corner of the church parking lot to a car detailer or small engine mechanic or their multipurpose room to a dance instructor or a local band that needs a place to practice? Could a Sunday school class gather $1,000 to present a zero-interest loan to a new entrepreneur who is unable to get a small business loan at a traditional financial institution but really needs to pay incorporation fees and get their website built?

In other words, churches focused on neighborhood revitalization help to free their communities from gentrification and other forms of expansion of dominant culture. An equity lens can help churches begin to imagine possibilities.

Power dynamics

If we are to create more equitable communities and institutions, we will have to understand the dynamics of power, who has access and who doesn't, who has voice and who doesn't, who is advantaged and who is disadvantaged, and where we fit on the spectrum of power. The anti-oppression power wheel shows the spectrum of power and oppression in a number of areas. It illustrates how it's possible to have advantage in certain areas while being disadvantaged or marginalized in other areas. As someone who is mostly on the power side of the spectrum, I (Shawn) have had to wrestle with what it means to hold power and what I can do about it.

In a seminary course on the history of racism and injustice, my professor Rick Gray, who is African American, educated us on the systemic aspects of race and also risked vulnerability and told us about his own personal wounds from racism. He shared the experience of meeting his white girlfriend's father for the first time. When he pulled up to the house, her dad met him in the driveway and slapped him in the face. When I heard the story, I felt the slap of racism in a way I had never felt before.

6.3 Anti-oppression power wheel[3]

At the end of the course, the room, mostly full of white males preparing to go into ministry, wanted to know one thing: "What are we supposed to do about our privilege?" Professor Gray could have said a lot of things. He could have said, "There's nothing you can do. You will always be spoiled, entitled white men." He could have made us feel guilty for the unearned privilege we ignorantly carried, or ashamed that we belonged to a cultural group that had imposed such an ugly racial system onto the world.

---

3. Adapted with permission from the Canadian Council for Refugees, http://ccrweb .ca/en/anti-oppression.

I had already been carrying a heavy load of white guilt, so it wouldn't have taken much to make me feel even worse. He could have slammed us, but he didn't. He looked at us with compassion and said, "You have a choice. You can use your privilege to climb the ladder and get as much as you can for yourself. Or you can use your privilege to open as many doors for others." He pointed the way to freedom, solidarity, and justice. His graceful invitation allowed me to pivot from guilt and shame to a sense of responsibility and a commitment to justice. I was empowered to act.

My life has never been the same since. I have learned over the years what it means to open doors of opportunity for others. It looks like creating more equitable spaces where everyone can bring their full selves, amplifying voices of those who are on the other end of the power spectrum, and looking for ways to share power and resources.

René August, a South African theologian and community developer we met on our racial justice pilgrimage to South Africa, said there are three things that justice leaders must do:

1. We must recognize our own privilege. When we think of ourselves as powerless, we become blind to the ways we abuse our power.
2. Give away power in preference to the Other. On the cross, Jesus deals a death blow to self-preservation.
3. Decide what we will do with our power even before we have it. Because when you wait until you have it, it's too late.[4]

No matter what social context we come from, we all hold power in some area. We have to decide what we will do with power. Will we ignore or hoard it? Or will we lay it down, leverage it, and share it?

Systems thinking
William Julius Wilson, in *More Than Just Race*, states that while individual and cultural factors play a role in outcomes for those in urban poverty, structural factors like politics and economics

---

4. René August, "Lead Change for Good" (plenary address, Christian Leadership Forum, Atlanta, GA, May 31, 2017).

play a far greater role.[5] Trying to modify individual or communal behavior may yield some results, but making structural changes will have a longer lasting and far greater reach.

I (Shawn) have learned I cannot love my neighbors without caring about the systems that are causing them harm. I saw how the prison system operates in our community. The prison system is devouring the lives and futures of so many young people and disproportionately affecting the poor.

So I became involved at a personal, or charity, level. I visited men in prison. I mentored youth with loved ones who were incarcerated. I gave gifts during the holidays to families who had a loved one in prison. I gave my time, my presence, and my resources.

Eventually I realized that I also needed to do community development. So I connected with organizations in which people were teaching classes, doing long-term mentoring, and connecting people to jobs. I got involved with Celestial Ministries, which has become a secondary family for children and families with incarcerated loved ones by providing music and academic support. The drumline of Celestial Ministries fights the cradle-to-prison pipeline by building a "cradle-to-drumline" pipeline that will lead kids into college. Several of our youth have gotten college scholarships to play drums.

This is development. It is good work, but this isn't enough. We have to go upstream and see what's causing mass incarceration in the first place. This has led me to be an advocate for prison reform—to speak up about the injustices within our prison system. There are many. Through this advocacy work, I have linked up with organizations that have the people power to devote to lobbying and advocacy efforts and keep the rest of us informed. I had to realize I couldn't end mass incarceration as an individual. If I were trying to address structural issues as an individual, I would either burn out or get depressed. It's difficult to bring change by ourselves. But there's strength in numbers. There is power in mass movement. Joining up with organizations, communities, and groups who share a similar passion and vision unleashes even greater potential for change.

---

5. William Julius Wilson, *More Than Just Race: Being Black and Poor in the Inner City* (New York: W. W. Norton, 2010), 135–36.

A friend recently said to me, "I see you doing advocacy. Have you seen any changes? Does it really make a difference?" I told him that a private prison was kept out of Crete, Illinois, because advocates in Little Village, a predominantly Latino community that stood to be the most adversely affected by it, and Crete, a predominantly white, wealthy community that didn't support this harmful privatized prison system, came together to fight and kept it out. I told him that I've seen churches rally together to hold police accountable. I've seen organizations fill in the gaps where government services and funding fall short while continuing to advocate for more equitable funding. I've seen people of faith unite across religious traditions to stand up against corporations that were exploiting workers.

The challenges are real and overwhelming at times. But I have seen firsthand that change is possible even in the most impossible situations.

Isolated impact versus collective impact

When individuals and organizations work independently from one another, they often do still manage to produce outputs. These outputs, or isolated impact markers, are rarely as comprehensive and sustainable, however, as those produced by collective impact. Collective impact occurs when people and organizations work together across sectors to develop cooperative, broad, and sustainable results. The chart illustrates the distinctions between isolated impact and collective impact.

While our organizations, Mission Year and Communities First Association, have historically focused on individual and community-level transformation, we started linking up with other organizations to address the systemic challenges affecting the contexts we serve. If we are going to address structural issues, we will need to collaborate with other organizations locally, nationally, and internationally that are committed to addressing root causes. Here are some exciting examples of such collaboration: Community Renewal Society is organizing churches in Chicago to act collectively for violence reduction and police accountability. Christian

6.4 Types of impact

Isolated impact	Collective impact
Funders select individual grantees that offer the most promising solutions	Funders and implementers understand that social problems, and their solutions, arise from the interaction of many organizations within a larger system
Organizations work separately and compete to produce the greatest independent impact	Organizations actively coordinate their actions and share lessons learned
Evaluation processes attempt to isolate a particular organization's impact	Progress depends on working toward the same goal and measuring the same things
Large-scale change is assumed to depend on scaling a single organization	Large-scale impact depends on increasing missional alignment and learning among many organizations
Corporate and government sectors are often disconnected from the efforts of foundations and smaller organizations	Corporate and government sectors are seen as potential partners

Community Development Association (CCDA), a network of evangelical churches and nonprofits, has made immigration, education, and mass incarceration top priorities in addition to their community development efforts in underresourced neighborhoods. World Relief is providing needed services for immigrants and refugees in the midst of anti-immigrant sentiments and reductions in refugee funding. Faith in Action (formerly PICO National Network), a network of faith-based community organizations, and the Live Free Campaign are mobilizing the faith community to add racial justice advocacy to their evangelism and mission priorities. Bread for the World is not only giving bread (charity) and education (development); it is also advocating for policies that will help end poverty globally (justice).

The collective impact of soul force is not limited to organizations. It can also be applied nationally and globally. Mahatma Gandhi and Martin Luther King channeled soul force for collective impact in India and the United States, respectively. Nelson Mandela implemented soul force into a national policy response to apartheid. Finland even devised a national identity around a concept resembling soul force called *sisu*: "a compound of bravery, ferocity, and tenacity, of the ability to keep fighting after most people would have quit, and to fight with the will to win."[6] While there is no pure English equivalent, *sisu* is characterized by resilience, conscientiousness, and grit. We would call it soul force. Whether effecting personal, communal, or systemic change, soul force is a source of power for transformation and collective impact.

SOUL FORCE STORY

From charity to change

Justin Tiarks

I was a teacher in an elementary school in Iowa before I spent a year in Chicago with Mission Year to learn how to merge my passion for teaching with my heart for social justice. Afterward I took a teaching job at a struggling school in Saint Paul, where I bring a community development and structural approach to issues that are often seen only through a charity lens.

I have been at the same school that I started at immediately after Mission Year. Since becoming principal, I have established something I call Vision 8/16. Distractions aside, what we really want for kids is eight great hours of school each day and sixteen great hours outside of school. This goal is accomplished by investing in two things: outstanding teachers and healthy families.

Our teacher investment has always been pivotal. The sad truth is, however, that it is not enough if we cannot engage the deeper systems of poverty, injustice, and racism that exist for kids outside of school.

---

6. Drake Baer, "This Untranslatable Finnish Word Takes Perseverance to a Whole New Level," *Business Insider*, June 17, 2014, http://www.businessinsider.com/finnish-word-sisu-is-key-to-success-2014-6.

Ninety-seven percent of our 480 kids live in poverty, and 60 percent are English learners. We are in the exciting process of building a community-based schools model. We are building a community center with a direct referral pipeline for all family needs: physical and mental health, job training, housing, immigration support, food, clothing, the works! Whatever barriers keep families from health, we want to be able to walk alongside them and knock these barriers down.

This dream started seven years ago, and we are now in the full process of realizing it. Blueprints and powerful, foundation-level partners have been secured. We are currently securing funding and contractors and look to begin our building in the next few months.

It is a myth that good instruction is all a kid needs. Kids also need a healthy family. We are "all in" to overcome challenges with our students and families. Too many places see challenges as too big and don't even try to address them. We see challenges and respond with big dreams. By supporting healthy systems for our kids, we hope to eradicate poverty for them in their lives and support them from surviving to thriving.

SOUL FORCE PIVOT POINTS

Create equitable spaces

When you are in groups, notice whose voice or perspective is missing. What is the composition of leadership teams, boards, and owners? Invite people to the table. Ask those in leadership why things are the way they are. Hold leaders and systems accountable around equity and justice.

Recognize your own power

If we are to create more equitable communities and institutions, we will have to understand the dynamics of power, who has access and who doesn't, who has voice and who doesn't, who is advantaged and who is disadvantaged, and where we fit on the spectrum of power. What power do you hold, and what will you do with it when you have it?

Share resources

We cannot have equity or justice if those with power are not willing to sacrifice privilege and share. What do you have in abundance that others desperately need? What are you willing to share? What makes sharing difficult for you? How can you leverage your own privilege to open doors of opportunity for others?

Work collectively

Who are people with whom you can link arms? What other organizations in your city or networks are also passionate about what you are passionate about? Link up with other individuals, communities, faith traditions, organizations, and causes to build greater movement.

Think structurally

What are some of the systems in your own life that you may take for granted because they are working for you? What systems are not working for you? What systems are not working for other people? How can you use a systems approach in your personal, work, or ministry context?

Support existing leaders

Who are the local, national, and global leaders who have been working for equity and justice for a long time? How can you encourage and support them? How can you partner with them and learn from them? Ask them for advice before you take action. Ask them how you can support their efforts.

PIVOT 6 MANTRA

Change involves individuals, communities, and systems.

Pivot 7

FROM MAINTENANCE
TO MOVEMENT

*Every moment is an organizing opportunity, every person a potential
activist, every minute a chance to change the world.*
—DOLORES HUERTA

While on a delegation trip to Guatemala with a group of
activist friends, I (Shawn) had the opportunity to visit the
La Puya community, a coalition of Indigenous people and allies
who were resisting the unlawful mining and contamination of
their water supply by a U.S. mining company. My friend Anton
Flores had heard about their struggle and suggested we join them
overnight. We pulled up to a makeshift compound on the side of
a one-lane dirt road. They had pieced together a barracks with a
covered kitchen and sleeping quarters out of discarded boards and
materials. On the opposite side of the road was a wooden plat-
form used for church services and community meetings. That was
where we would end up sleeping that night as big chicken buses
and semitrucks whizzed by on the way to the Tambor mine site.

The La Puya community greeted us warmly and offered us food
and drink. We sat down with a matriarch of the community who
shared the story of their movement.

It had started with a single act of nonviolent resistance. A woman concerned by the sudden arrival of the mining operation in her community parked her car sidewise along the narrow dirt road to block the path. Others, inspired by her courage, joined her to block the tractors, dump trucks, and other equipment from getting by.

This human roadblock became the La Puya resistance movement, and the group committed to peacefully protest at this site for as long as it would take. Eventually, an armed security force was sent to forcibly remove them. The women in the community decided to go on the frontlines, thinking that the armed guards would go easier on them. But the guards did not hold back. They shot tear gas canisters at them and removed them with physical force.

The community rallied and decided that it was too dangerous to confront the guards. Instead, they committed to stand vigil at the entrance to the mining company round the clock in protest against their actions and to remind the company that they were not backing down. They divided up into groups and took shifts along the roadside into the entrance. Meanwhile, they were also working through legal channels to try to block the mining company. During their shifts they prayed, they sang, they played cards, they ate food, they laughed, and they encouraged one another.

The matriarch was knitting the whole time she shared the story with us. She stopped to show us the scars on her body from where she had been hit by the canisters during the raid. But throughout the story she had an unspeakable joy on her face that didn't make sense given her circumstances. When I found out they had been keeping vigil nonstop for four years, I was completely stunned. We slept outside that night, but I couldn't sleep at all. I was in awe of this brazen display of communal soul force.

That week they just so happened to have won a major victory in the Guatemalan Supreme Court, which declared the actions of the mining company to be illegal. We marched with them through the city to celebrate and to rally outside the Supreme Court. Even though they won that day, the people in the movement knew that the company would likely not comply. We asked what we could do to help, and they told us to tell their story.

I have learned so much about movement from the La Puya community and other movement makers who refuse to give up in the face of forces of despair and injustice. When we discover soul force, and when we pivot from fear and lies to freedom and truth, we see movement. The movement generated from soul force can be large, earth-shaking movement. But movement is often a succession of small, steady motions that build momentum over time.

The beauty and power of Niagara Falls is awe inspiring. If you trace the path of the river back before it reaches the edge of the falls, however, you find something that may be surprising. When you isolate the river in your view so that you cannot see the falls at all, it looks like a calm river in which nothing is happening. The farther away you look from the actual falls, the slower the river seems to be moving.

But just because you can't see the river moving doesn't mean it's not. The current is moving slowly but steadily in the direction of the falls. The dramatic change—the tourist attraction—is the falls. But the falls come after a long-term, consistent, and sometimes invisible motion.

Once we pivot in the right direction, we tap into a powerful current that creates movement in our lives and builds over time into a dynamic force for change. While we must not lose sight of the larger systemic issues in need of change, big changes usually start with small, consistent action over a long period of time. Enduring change hinges upon our ability to live out our activism deeply and collaboratively!

Soul force is like a current flowing toward individual and collective movement. We have highlighted some of the dams that block soul force from flowing like a mighty river in our lives, organizations, and world. But there is one more we have to address, one that is more subtle than some of the other factors, yet equally troublesome.

The urge toward maintenance can block the free flow of passion and purpose that keeps movement alive. Maintenance is the preservation of status quo living. It's contentment with the way things are. Maintenance means accepting mediocrity when greatness and brilliance is possible. It's easy for individuals and institutions to get stuck in maintenance mode. When we are operating from a place of self-centeredness, we can obsess about our own survival rather than the survival of us all.

MAINTENANCE IS GOOD; MOVEMENT IS GREAT

In the book *Good to Great*, James Collins argues that we often settle for what is good rather than pushing toward what is great. "Good is the enemy of great. And that is one of the key reasons why we have so little that becomes great," Collins writes. "We don't have great schools, principally because we have good schools. We don't have great government, principally because we have good government. Few people attain great lives, in large part because it is just so easy to settle for a good life."[1] Maintenance is about settling for good when we could be great.

Right now, many older denominational churches are dying because they are stuck in maintenance mode. They are married to one way of doing things. They have lost their fire, their purpose for being. We know many churches that are more focused on maintaining old buildings than creating new ministries. The churches that are growing are the ones able to adapt to change and become more relevant to the people and context where they are placed. Many denominations are rolling out new churches that hold more loosely to their denominational affiliation. Instead of insisting on the *form* of church (maintenance), leaders are becoming more invested in the *substance* of church (movement), and they are allowing the substance to take on local expressions.

It's important to state that maintenance, in and of itself, is not a bad thing. Some maintenance—in individuals, organizations, and churches—is always required. But maintenance cannot be

1. James Collins, *Good to Great: Why Some Companies Make the Leap . . . and Others Don't* (New York: HarperBusiness, 2001), 1.

mistaken for the movement. Remaining in maintenance mode can hold individuals and organizations back from innovation, creativity, depth, and collective change. Maintenance is often motivated by the same lies and fears that marked the other pivots. In the same way that making the seven pivots leads to movement, refusing to make the pivots leads to maintenance. Ultimately, maintenance leads to stunted growth and death.

FOURTEEN MARKS OF MOVEMENT

Soul force leads us to movement over maintenance, to living fully over just getting by, to emphasizing the substance over the form. The following table outlines fourteen ways that maintenance and movement come into conflict in our personal lives and institutions, and the pivots we can make to choose movement over maintenance.

7.1 Maintenance versus movement

	Maintenance	Movement
Spiritual impulse	Legalism	Love
Religious emphasis	Ritual	Renewal
Social interaction	Transactional	Transformational
Organizational priority	Corporation focused	Cause focused
Vocational motivation	Paycheck and career	Purpose and calling
Power posture	Political: seeking power	Prophetic: speaking truth to power
Change stance	Status quo	Subversive
Justice leaning	Law and order	Liberation
Management style	Controlling	Coaching and curating
Growth tendency	Mediocrity	Maturity and mastery
Financial concern	Stewardship	Social equity
Calculated risk	Risk averse	Risk-taking
Means of production	Product (the ends justify the means)	Process (the ends do not justify the means)
Primary driver	"Grass tips" and top down	Grass roots and bottom up

1. Love as the driving force

When our focus is maintenance—whether in families or organizations or religious institutions—we tend toward legalism instead of love. When an idea or dream begins, it is usually with a great deal of excitement and passion. But inevitably, the energy of the vision gives way to the mundane details and tasks of maintenance, and the motivation for the dream becomes lost.

For families, this can look like a father who works diligently to provide the basic necessities for his family but never tells his children he loves them. For churches, this occurs when the spiritual impulse becomes caught up in legalism rather than love, and when monitoring people's behavior becomes more important than setting captives free. For organizations, this occurs when the reason for existing becomes maintaining systems rather than accomplishing mission. For athletes, it happens when they lose the love of the game amid the business of the game.

Sustaining movement is about keeping love central. When E. Stanley Jones asked Mahatma Gandhi what Christian missionaries in India could do to make the gospel more palatable, Gandhi told him, "Emphasize love and make it your working force, for love is central to Christianity."[2] Love was central in the life and work of Jesus. He urged his followers to keep love for God and love for neighbor at the center of their individual and collective lives. So often the church is seen as a legalistic community rather than a loving one. The heart of soul force is love. When love is the driving force in our lives, movement follows.

2. The fire of renewal

If the spiritual impetus of soul force is love over legalism, then the religious emphasis is renewal over ritual. In the New Testament, renewal is tied to transformation: "Be transformed by the renewing of your minds" (Romans 12:2). The emphasis of Christian faith should not be ritual or rote memorization or acting religious. Following Christ means entering into a process of being renewed.

---

2. E. Stanley Jones, *Gandhi: An Interpretation* (Nashville: Abingdon-Cokesbury Press, 1948), 51.

Renewal has multiple meanings. It can mean to make new (restore); to take up again (resume); to repeat so as to reaffirm; to regain or restore the physical or mental vigor of (revive); to replenish; and to bring into being again (reestablish).[3] Consider what might happen if the emphasis of our religious life was to restore what's been hurt and broken in our lives through the love and grace of Christ; to resume life-giving activities that make us and others come alive in our calling; to repeat and reaffirm truths that remind us who we are as children of God and what we are capable of as image bearers; to develop practices and rhythms that sustain our faith and hope in the midst of injustice; to replenish our weary souls; and to reestablish who we were meant to be and who we have always dreamed of becoming.

Renewal is a dynamic process that brings life and love and movement. Rituals can aid us in the process of renewal, but they cannot be an end in themselves. When the religious emphasis becomes performing rituals alone, our faith dies. To put it another way, if ritual is the candle, renewal is the flame. You need a candle to have the flame, but without the flame, the candle is useless. When renewal becomes the emphasis, then we light a fire in ourselves and others.

3. Transformational relationships

When we are in maintenance mode, our relationships can end up being more transactional than transformational. Transactional relationships tend to be impersonal and often serve a specific agenda. An example of a transactional relationship might be an interaction in line at a grocery store or commercial business, where goods or services are exchanged with little human connection.

Transformational relationships, on the other hand, are personal, mutual relationships with genuine human connection. A transformational relationship can be initiated by a customer who takes time to ask a worker how their day has been, or a worker who wants to know more about you than your order. Teshauna works the register at a local café on the West Side of Chicago that we

3. *The Free Dictionary*, s.v. "renew," accessed January 16, 2018, https://www.thefree dictionary.com/renew.

both frequent. She has an energy and smile that is contagious. She not only knows how to make a good cup of coffee, but takes joy in connecting with people who come into the café. When she isn't working a particular shift, we feel a different atmosphere in the room. Teshauna's passion for people transforms the impersonal exchange into a dynamic encounter of grace. For her, community, not coffee, is the point of the café.

Transformational relationships put people at the center of our life, work, ministry, and hospitality.

4. Cause focused

Neither of us are natural fundraisers. We don't enjoy asking people for money. We are grassroots ministry people, not corporate business folks. But we both knew we needed to do something if our organizations were going to stay alive.

For the first couple of months of leadership at our organizations, both of us did what executive directors do: we dressed up, met with major donors, and begged them to support our work. But for some reason, it didn't feel right. Like David trying to fit into Saul's armor, it just didn't work. We were trying to force a plan that was not our own.

We learned that organizations focused on their own maintenance are not as effective as organizations that focus on their cause. Not many people get excited about maintaining an organization, but people do get excited about getting behind a cause they believe in. We realized that our job as executive directors was not asking people for money to keep our organizations afloat; rather, our work was educating people about our organizations' missions. In ministry terms, our main role was to disciple people in our cause of God's love and justice for the city.

This revolutionized our leadership. Both of us learned that wearing suits and coercing a transaction is not our deal. But discipling people and sojourning toward community transformation and justice? We're all in!

At the end of the day, what we remember will not be how many emails we sent or dollars we raised; it will be the relationships we've made and the lives we affected. Maintenance is necessary. Balancing budgets is important. But we thrive as individuals and as organizations by living, moving, and creating change.

5. Purpose over paycheck

When we live for the movement, our vocational motivation is purpose over paycheck. To make the shift from maintenance to movement, we have to tap into something greater than ourselves to find a cause and to live out our purpose. We find purpose when we use our gifts in service to humanity. When we make decisions solely on financial security or a paycheck, we often grow discontent. The ultimate is to get paid for what we love doing. Sometimes we have to do what we don't love to pay the bills. Fulfillment isn't in a paycheck but in purpose. Maintenance, driven by a consumer mindset, keeps us preoccupied with paychecks. Movement, driven by creativity, shifts our focus to purpose. Money concerns are real and important, but when they drive every decision, we lose sight of what true value and significance is.

What will define your life? Will it be the titles you collect and the positions of power you hold? Or will it be the ways you serve humanity and touch lives along the way?

6. Prophetic: Speaking truth to power

Maintenance is political by nature and is focused on preserving the status quo. Maintenance favors the current political structures and hierarchies. Movement, on the other hand, is prophetic. Movement speaks truth to power rather than seeking power for its own ends.

Prophets, in the Hebrew Scriptures and in modern history, feel a responsibility to call out abuses of power. Rabbi Abraham Heschel, in *The Prophets*, talks about the pathos of God. Heschel believed the prophets not only spoke for God; they shared God's divine concern for humanity.[4] They felt what God felt about injustice and spoke from that feeling. In *The Prophetic Imagination*, Walter Brueggemann makes a distinction between the royal consciousness

---

4. On Heschel's theology of the pathos of God, see Abraham J. Heschel, *The Prophets* (New York: Harper and Row, 1962), 285–98.

of Solomon, which functioned to maintain the social order, and
the prophetic imagination of Moses, who set out to topple the
whole exploitive system.[5] Movement makers are prophetic and
have prophetic imagination. They share God's divine concern for
humanity, and they are more loyal to truth, love, and justice than
to preserving power structures.

7. Subversion of the status quo

Movement makers shake up social systems that privilege power
relationships, economic profit, and military might. There can be
no movement without challenging unjust social systems. If maintenance is business as usual, movement is a total disruption of the
business apparatus. Movement requires flipping tables, because
the scales are rigged, the playing fields are uneven, and the decks
are stacked toward the rich and powerful.

Movement leaders question sacred cows within their religious,
political, and economic life. They subvert the status quo and live
according to the way the world ought to be rather than the way it
is. They seek to live on earth as it is in heaven. They unearth what
those in power would rather keep hidden. They speak inconve-
nient truths. Because of this, they face extra opposition and they
catch a lot of flack.

Father Michael Pfleger, priest of Saint Sabina Catholic Church
in Chicago, is a prophetic leader. He speaks out about gun violence, challenges police, and confronts politicians. In a course for
students at Yale University, he encouraged them to "be a thorn in
the side of those in power. People ought to wake up pissed off that
you exist because you make them feel uncomfortable and dissatis-
fied with the status quo."

8. Justice that liberates

Justice for those in maintenance mode looks like law and order.
The dominant culture doesn't desire or understand true justice.

---

5. The contrast between prophetic imagination and royal consciousness runs through-
out the book, but for initial analysis and definitions of each, see Walter Brueggemann,
"The Alternative Community of Moses" and "Royal Consciousness: Countering the
Counterculture," chaps. 1 and 2 in *The Prophetic Imagination* (Minneapolis: Fortress
Press, 2001).

To those in step with the dominant culture, justice means locking up people who transgress the social norms and cultural customs. Their God is a God of order, not a God of justice for the oppressed.

According to the King James Version of the Bible, Jesus said, "Blessed are they which do hunger and thirst after righteousness: for they shall be filled" (Matthew 5:6). The Greek word for "righteousness" means both righteousness and justice. To hunger and thirst for justice has a much different connotation than hunger and thirst for righteousness.

Some biblical scholars believe the word in this verse was intentionally translated as *righteousness*. King James, under whose reign the translation was written, did not want his people hungering and thirsting for *justice*, which might have made them consider overthrowing him. But he would have had no problem having *righteous* citizens who obeyed the law, went to work, and paid their taxes.

For many people, justice equates to personal righteousness and obeying laws rather than liberation for those who are suffering and oppressed. For movement makers, justice looks like hungering and thirsting for what could be, what should be, and what must be: liberation for all.

9. Coaching people and curating spaces

For leaders and managers stuck in maintenance mode, methods of leadership become controlling rather than coaching and curating. For movement makers, leadership isn't about controlling people but about curating spaces where people can thrive and become who they are meant to be.

People in a movement are responsible for its progress, and people are much more effective when they actually believe something themselves rather than simply being *told* what to believe or aspire to. This work requires a trust that each person's soul force will be activated in a way that allows for discovery that is appropriate and timely. We must be true *servant leaders* in this work: relinquishing what we *think* a person needs to know for the desire to witness the manifestation of what the soul knows.

10. Maturity and long-term growth

Maintenance is the plateau for growth. Maintenance fosters mediocrity. When we are holding ourselves and others accountable to love and liberation, we are constantly being challenged to grow deeper. Maturity and mastery come with steadiness and persistence. As Malcolm Gladwell has noted, mastery requires ten thousand hours of practice.[6] That is the amount of time that allows for expert status. Community development leaders John Perkins and Wayne "Coach" Gordon frequently assert that if you want to make a difference in the life of a young person in the city (or elsewhere), you need to commit to at least fifteen years. Maturity and mastery come with long-term commitment and persistence.

What's radical nowadays is not doing something extreme for a weekend or a year. What's radical is being consistent over time. Movement breeds maturity and long-term growth.

11. Commitment to social equity

In the last chapter, we talked about the importance of equity. If we are operating in maintenance mode, we might be stewarding an unjust system. It wasn't enough for Christian slaveholders to steward their resources or treat their slaves fairly; they were missing a social equity and justice lens. We need to not only steward our resources; we need to move toward equitable social arrangements. Movement makers are constantly evaluating systems to see where things are inequitable.

To do this well as leaders, we must invest time and money in training and professional development around cultivating an equity lens. We need to commit to learning about social equity just as we would any other aspect of our leadership capacity. Additionally, developing true relationships with people who already have skill capacity in areas like race and gender equity will support our organic development in this area.

---

6. For more on the ten-thousand-hour rule, see Malcolm Gladwell, *Outliers: The Story of Success* (New York: Little, Brown and Company), 35–68. Gladwell credits Daniel J. Levitin for originating this concept in *This Is Your Brain on Music: The Science of a Human Obsession* (New York: Dutton, 2006), 197.

12. Risk-taking

Movement makers are risk-takers. They step out of their comfort zones, they activate their faith, and they take chances. Maintenance people tend to manage liabilities by minimizing risk, which often results in preserving existing structures rather than creating new initiatives. Risk-takers are often visionaries. They are willing to step out even when they are afraid. Their excitement about the vision, however, can sometimes cause them to fail to count the cost. Risk-takers need strong, supportive people who can help them take calculated risks.

There is an important correlation between faith and risk-taking. We often talk about having faith, keeping the faith, and activating our faith, but we don't often live our lives in ways that require us to have faith. We focus on activities that keep us safe, and we only invest in those things that are sure and certain. This way of living does not require us to tap into our soul force. It is only when we reach beyond what we have the capacity to do on our own that we can tap into our reservoir of faith and hope. It is only when we seek things that require more than we have to give as individuals that we can flourish collectively. The risk is in trusting beyond what we see in ourselves and in depending on our community to bring about flourishing for all.

13. Process as important as product

For movement people, process is as important as product. How we get there is as important as where we end up. For Mahatma Gandhi and Martin Luther King, nonviolent means were as critical as the nonviolent ends. Violence breeds violence, and hatred breeds hatred. King famously said, "Hate cannot drive out hate; only love can do that."[7] Violent means cannot lead to peaceful ends. Maintenance is more concerned about products, while movement is more concerned about process.

As a white person engaged in racial justice, I (Shawn) am discovering that the process is much more important than the product.

---

7. Martin Luther King, "Where Do We Go from Here: Chaos or Community?," in *A Testament of Hope: The Essential Writings and Speeches*, ed. James M. Washington (San Francisco: HarperCollins, 1986), 594.

If I only think about the product and maintaining my own career, I can allow myself to become a white voice speaking on behalf of people of color and underserved communities. But if I become the voice, then I am perpetuating the system as it is. Even though I am speaking about racism and justice, I am still maintaining a system in which white voices are elevated over marginalized voices.

I realized this when Reesheda and I attended the prayer vigil for Laquan McDonald. A news reporter was walking around and asking people for their thoughts on why we were there. As an internal processor, I hate being put on the spot, and I really don't like video cameras. I also knew Reesheda would have much better things to say than me. So I encouraged the reporter to interview her. Reesheda gave a brilliant assessment of the issue of violence and the need for police accountability in Chicago. After she was done, the reporter also interviewed me, and I managed to piece together a few words. But on the news that night, they played a clip of me and not Reesheda.

Since then, I have made a concerted effort to focus on the process over the product. Part of the process for me, as someone from the dominant culture, is to do more things in partnership. For me, this looks like coleading, cofacilitating workshops, coauthoring a book, and cospeaking. This allows the audience to hear other voices and perspectives and checks my white, dominant voice. An unexpected outcome has been that it has removed a lot of the stress and anxiety I used to feel when speaking, and it has brought more joy. This also means that sometimes the process takes longer. But in the end, the collaborative product is multidimensional and more beautifully diverse.

14. Grassrooted

The primary driver of maintenance is the "grass tips": strategies, policies, and agencies that operate from the top down. In this way, maintenance mode "maintains" power structures instead of transforming them. People in power at the grass tips have a stake in the system as it is, and they can sometimes feel threatened by movements that are working toward change.

The primary driver of movement is the grass roots. Movement catalyzes from the bottom up. Most social movements arise from the grass roots, because it is those at the root of a community who feel the impact most and who bear an unfair weight of the burdens of social systems. This doesn't mean change cannot come via institutions and people in positions of power. But the urgency for change usually comes from those at the bottom who make enough noise to be heard or who force the hand of those at the grass tips.

For example, President Lyndon Johnson is credited with signing the Civil Rights Act of 1964. But it took almost a decade of organizing, boycotts, and sit-ins at the grassroots level to move him to act.

If we are leaders at the grass tips, it is imperative that we listen to the critiques from those at the grass roots and margins. Movement makers stay connected to the grass roots even if they are elevated into positions at the grass tips.

But what about the "grass stalks," or the "grass middle?" The grass middle are those in the middle class who are neither power brokers at the grass tips nor oppressed agents of change at the grass roots. The grass middle holds the tips and the roots in place. They are the ones who actually keep the structures in place.

In *Rules for Radicals*, Saul Alinsky talks about the trinity of class distinctions: the Haves; the Have-Nots; and the Have-a-Little; Want Mores.[8] The Have-a-Little, Want Mores represent this grass middle. They stretch upward toward the tips. Fear of scarcity, class barriers, consumerism, self-centeredness, resentment and hurt, charity, and maintenance keep the Have-a-Little, Want Mores in place and weaken their connection with the grass roots. But Alinsky also points out that many movement leaders come from this middle group, because they are close enough to those on the grass roots to see their struggles but also close enough to the grass tips to leverage power and demand change.

Moses is a good biblical example of this. As a Hebrew, he was able to empathize with the struggle of the enslaved Hebrews. As

---

8. Saul Alinsky, *Rules for Radicals: A Practical Primer for Realistic Radicals* (New York: Vintage Books, 1989), 18–23.

a member of the royal Egyptian family, he was also familiar with the ruling powers and pressures. This position made him a perfect advocate for the Hebrew people.

Whatever position we find ourselves in, we can support movement for change if we stay committed at the grass roots, leverage our position, and apply steady pressure on those at the grass tips to act in the interest of everyone.

COMMITMENT FOR THE LONG HAUL: PIVOT TO MOVEMENT

The journey to movement is long. Nelson Mandela said, "The struggle is my life."[9] So many people who have overcome their fears and entered into solidarity with people have given their lives to the causes they believe in. They have become movement makers because they have made soul force a way of life.

We want to share some contemporary examples of what it looks like to be movement makers in families, communities, churches, and businesses.

Family as a movement

Bryan and Christin Babcock live in Rochester, New York, where they are intentionally living in community and pursuing a lifestyle of justice as a family. On a recent visit, I (Shawn) was able to visit with them and see their community up close. They have purposefully chosen to root themselves in a disadvantaged neighborhood and weave their lives together with the lives of their neighbors.

When I asked what their goal was, they responded, "We are just trying to be." They aren't trying to accomplish something great. They are simply building community, and although it's messy and chaotic at times, it appears to be natural and effortless for them.

I tagged along with Bryan for a weekly guys' breakfast at a local Black-owned business. The owner knew their names and what they were going to order. He thanked them for coming and said, "It's customers like you who have come in every week for

---

9. Nelson Mandela, "The Struggle Is My Life," chap. 4 in *Long Walk to Freedom: The Autobiography of Nelson Mandela* (Boston: Back Bay Books, 1996).

the last four years that keep this place going." Children from the neighborhood came into their backyard to play on their trampoline and to play with the Babcocks' kids. Christin treats the kids like her own. While they are in her backyard, they are loved, nurtured, and reminded of the ground rules.

When the Babcocks heard about an unaccompanied minor who had found his way into the United States, they didn't hesitate to take him in and welcome him into their family. During my visit he was still learning English and adjusting to his new context, but he was happy to be in a safe place.

Throughout the weekend, the Babcocks sat on neighbors' porches, borrowed tables, and shared meals. They send their kids to public schools, because they want them to go to school with kids who are different from them. Their oldest son appreciates his parents' choices and sees the benefit of the lifestyle his parents have chosen. He was part of a soccer team that made national news when they knelt during the national anthem to protest police brutality against unarmed Black men, women, and children. He was interviewed on television and said he did it to support his Black teammates.

Additionally, Bryan and his friend Austin started a bee collective, Sweet Beez, Inc., which is dedicated to fostering a stronger honeybee population in the city of Rochester and El Sauce, Guatemala. They educate and empower communities with new economic and social capital, and advocate for policies that work to fight against climate change and for immigration justice.

The Babcocks show us what movement looks like for a family. They show us it's possible to be responsible parents yet still pursue values we care about. They are living with purpose, but it doesn't feel forced, and it isn't driven by guilt. They aren't trying to maintain some standard of justice they read about in a book. They are simply making a series of pivots that have opened them to find their purpose as a family in community, solidarity, and justice.

Faith as a social movement
What if we could recover the church as a social movement? After all, the church began as a revolutionary movement, not as an

institution to be maintained. It wasn't until the time of Constantine that the church became institutionalized and more interested in maintenance than movement. But the church can still be a force for change if it recovers its roots as a dynamic social movement. One way we are trying to do this is by reimagining church and recovering church as a community, not just a building.

Hope Brock is a faith leader at Church on the Block (COTB) in Austin, one of Chicago's largest and most intentionally disadvantaged neighborhoods. In a conversation with us, she illustrated what church as a social movement looks like.

> "Church on the Block, for as long as I have known it to be, has understood itself to be a community of people who come together to worship and sabbath once a week, then go out and be the church throughout the rest of the week all around Chicago's West Side." That's how Lau Torres, one of our church leaders, has always so eloquently and accurately said it.
>
> This coming together weekly may look celebratory, including singing songs that give God the highest praise. It may look like lamenting together when someone in the community has experienced loss or in response to the realities for our neighborhood or nation that week. It sometimes looks like reading Scripture and remembering God's provision and promise, or being made uncomfortable by a sermon that reminds us who God calls God's people to be. Other times, it looks like a place of rest when the previous week has been long or heavy or when the needs for ourselves or others feel too great.
>
> The going out and being the church throughout the week often looks like dinner with neighbors, mentoring a teen, gathering with people to do art and be creative, listening to the story of another, showing up for others in times of transition and loss, running a local neighborhood school, being a moving crew at a moment's notice, throwing a community movie night, celebrating birthdays, checking in on neighbors who have seen or experienced violence, fleshing out a new business venture, creating space, holding tension, participating in a protest, creating dialogue between Chicago police and Austin teens, resolving conflict, sitting in a coaching session, or apartment hunting.

The list could go on and on, but what I began to realize early on was that the community of COTB was not merely a weekly moment or a gathering. Rather, COTB is a movement that feels and is bigger than me, bigger than each person individually. A movement that is very much a kingdom work and a daily participation with the holy. It's a people who understands itself best when it is doing, caring for, being present with, and engaging. Even when the doing is hard, heavy, painful, or shaping (which it often is), the movement continues.

Business as a social movement

One of the exciting shifts in the business world is the pivot to using business as a means for social change. Many businesses are becoming companies "for purpose" and not just for profit. Consequently, entrepreneurs have been tying their business savvy to their social justice priorities.

Shelby Parchman, president of the board of directors for Communities First Association, is no stranger to such innovation. Often celebrated for the way he coaches budding entrepreneurs in their start-up endeavors, Parchman emphasizes the importance of ensuring that new business owners not only consider what they want their businesses to produce. Rather, Parchman challenges new start-ups to connect with the community and the business's target market to determine what that demographic wants, needs, or would benefit from having in the community. Parchman encourages entrepreneurs to listen to the community to determine what the felt and expressed needs of that community are, and then to serve by providing goods and services that are in line with the holistic development of that community. This is a definitive paradigm shift: from the business owner driving the industry to the business owner listening to the community about how to most effectively be of service.

Because so few sustainable businesses have been started among traditionally underserved communities, and because of the vast impact that businesses in intentionally marginalized neighborhoods have on the community's economy, Parchman coaches and supports entrepreneurs who are emerging from these communities.

His own willingness to respond to the economic crisis in these communities has resulted in a flourishing coaching practice for Parchman, as well as the emergence of several successful business owners within those communities. This is what business as a social movement produces: multiple layers of growth and development for the individuals and the collectives associated with these initiatives.

When we are movement-minded, everything in our lives begins to align with our deepest values and convictions. Our lives become endowed with greater purpose. Soul force transforms our souls, yes, but it also transforms every other aspect of our lives, as well as the lives around us.

EIGHT KEY SUSTAINABILITY PRACTICES

When you tap into your soul force and begin to align your life with your values, you will find an extra energy within you. But you will also be drawn to more and more activity. It's important that we also tend to our souls as we act in the world. If we want to sustain the movement, it will be important to cultivate sustainable practices.

Here are some practices that have helped other movement makers sustain themselves over the long haul.

1. Find rest

Take deep breaths. Take a nap. Slow down. Pace yourself. Stress is an enemy to sustainability. When we don't rest, we often hold stress within our bodies. We each find rest differently, so find the things that make you feel rested, and do them regularly.

2. Take care of your body

The older we get, the more important it is to take care of our bodies. If we want to be in the work for the long haul, we need our bodies. The power of soul force is connected to the longevity of the body. Drinking water, focusing on good nutrition, getting enough sleep, and being physically active help sustain us over the long haul.

3. Acknowledge both your light and shadow sides

We often think of people as good or evil, but the reality is that we all have light and shadow sides. Instead of creating binaries between good people (us) and bad people (them), acknowledge your light and shadow sides. This gives us more humility, understanding, and compassion for others. It also keeps us from becoming self-righteous and reactionary.

4. Do what brings you life

What do you do to restore your soul? Sometimes we get so busy in the work that it becomes easy for the outer work of peace to overshadow the inner work of peace. Sustaining ourselves requires taking time to do what brings life. This could be reading, writing, running, watching movies, meeting up with friends at a coffee shop, or walking in a local park.

5. Learn when to say no and when to say yes

Movement makers know when to say no to what's good in order to say yes to what's best. Needs are always around us. Practicing discernment and setting boundaries will allow us to protect ourselves from burnout and help keep us on mission.

6. Form community and collaborate

Forming community is just as subversive and sustainable as organizing rallies. When we go to rallies, we try to bring someone else along. When you run alone, it is easier to get tired and want to quit. But running with a pack will keep you motivated to continue in times of doubt and despair. Activism isn't enough to sustain our souls; we were made for community and collaboration.

7. Find a mentor or coach for lifelong learning

Having a mentor or coach allows us to continue discovering ourselves while we are working on changing the world. Mentors provide perspective and insights that we may not see and hold us accountable to many of the practices we have mentioned here. Having a coach can help us harness our learning and develop more capacity for courage, community, and change than we would otherwise.

8. Commit to the long haul

When we commit to the movement for the long haul, we are able to take time for ourselves without feeling guilty. We are able to take breaks and rest, and we give ourselves time to develop our capacities and gifts to create a sustained and lasting impact. Change takes time. We need time to develop. Committing for the long haul allows us to make a lifetime of change.

WHAT WILL BE REMEMBERED?

In the end, we won't remember how many likes we had on Facebook posts, how many emails we sent, or how much money we had in our bank accounts. It will be the relationships we built, the moments of transformation we experienced, the lives that we were able to affect, and the movements for change we were part of.

Why just maintain systems when you can transform them? Why settle for maintenance when you can inspire movement?

SOUL FORCE STORY

From maintenance to movement

One of the greatest stories of movement making has not been celebrated to the extent that it should be. The dedication, commitment, sacrifice, and passion that Dolores Huerta exhibited in her fight for the rights of farmworkers is the standard to bear toward justice.

As cofounder of the National Farmworkers Association (later to become United Farm Workers), Huerta committed her life to the equitable treatment of farmers of color who worked under brutal and inhumane conditions.

Laying aside her passion for dance, Huerta became an activist, organizer, and labor union leader who committed her life to the cause and galvanized communities across the United States. She did this during a time in which it was considered unacceptable for women to be vocal and assertive. Perpetually criticized for redefining the framework for motherhood, Huerta served alongside Cesar Chavez for decades, although she never received the recognition and accolades that he did.

Huerta lobbied politicians, organized Spanish-language voting ballots, fought for accommodations for Spanish speakers to take driver's education, and successfully negotiated contracts for the union to establish quality working conditions for immigrant farmers, including the reduction of the use of harmful pesticides.

In 1988, Huerta was almost beaten to death by San Francisco police officers while at a protest rally, yet even that travesty did not silence this rallying voice for justice. Huerta and her children now lead the Dolores Huerta Foundation, which ensures that other voices for the movement are developed and supported.

When asked what she would have done differently as a part of her role in the farmworkers' movement, Huerta once said that she would have worked harder at loving her enemies and having grace for those who did not yet understand the severity of the issues.

This is the heart of a movement maker, and we give honor to her work, her life, and the movement she inspired.

SOUL FORCE PIVOT POINTS

Keep love central

Make love your driving force. Elevate love over ideology. When other priorities become the focus of your faith community, family, organization, or social network, reprioritize by always drawing people back to love.

Pursue your purpose

Use your gifts in service to humanity. Look for ways to get paid for what you love to do. Root for your purpose!

Take calculated risks

Be willing to take a chance on the people, passion, and purpose of your life and the lives around you.

Stay connected to the grass roots

Whether you are positioned at the grass roots, grass tips, or somewhere in between, stay connected with the grass roots. Find ways to leverage your position and power in support of the grass-roots movement.

Incorporate sustainable practices

Do the work of learning what works! Glean from other leaders, and witness the work in other places to learn best practices from people not like you. Be willing to forego traditional but ineffective practices in order to incorporate lasting innovations.

PIVOT 7 MANTRA

In love we live and move.

THE JOURNEY
CONTINUES

Love isn't passive. It is an active force, a galvanizing energy for justice and true peace.
—BERNICE A. KING

You have made it to the end of the book, and now the real journey begins! Let's look back at where we've been and where we have yet to go.

Soul force pivots are not one-time acts but a way of life. Remember: it's about the journey, not the destination. When we make the pivots, we make the movement. When the pivots align, something powerful is unleashed—something that has been there, inside each of us, all along. Gandhi called it *satyagraha*. King called it soul force. Christ called it the kingdom of God that is within us (Luke 17:21).

With our community, we may be in the middle of one pivot: from charity to change. In our relationship with a parent, we might be moving from hurt to hope. In our working life, we may be somewhere between maintenance and movement.

We have identified seven pivots to apply to different areas of our lives—each one small when taken in isolation, and each one powerful when taken collectively in a movement for change. We have accepted the continual, perpetual nature of the pivots, recognizing that we may have to revisit each one from time to time.

Pivot 1: We have confronted our fears. We have named them. We have become aware of how fear makes us believe lies that do not bring freedom. We have made pivots from the lies of fear to the truths of freedom. The journey ahead is to keep choosing freedom.

Pivot 2: We have begun to identify barriers built by fear and intentionally moved toward building bridges. We have committed to dialogue over debate. We have opened our minds to difference, recognizing that diversity is a strength. We are welcoming, not building walls. The journey ahead lies in dismantling the barriers and bridging the divides.

Pivot 3: We have recognized our self-centeredness as human nature. We have embraced that we are each a part connected to a greater whole, and that what affects one affects us all. We have thought about the impact of our actions on others. We have considered ways to link up with others and stand with people in their pain, making the community stronger. The journey ahead is to see, know, and acknowledge people and to strengthen the bonds of solidarity with all humanity.

Pivot 4: We have unearthed hurts so that we can pursue the path of healing. We have faced our trauma, recognized righteous indignation, and engaged in lament. We have sought forgiveness for ourselves and others and committed to nonviolent resistance and hope-filled resilience. We have realized that hope is one of the greatest weapons against injustice. The journey ahead means continuing to acknowledge our pain and nourish our hope, as they are both ever present with us.

Pivot 5: We have acknowledged our consumer mindset and realized our need to develop a creative mindset. We have received the call to resist being passive consumers and embraced our identity as active creators, made in the image of God. We have acknowledged our creative power and our potential as artistic activists. Our journey now lies in resisting the pull of consumerism and nurturing the need for creativity to reimagine our world.

Pivot 6: We have explored different models of change. We have seen that charity is not enough, and that community development and justice are critical. We have wrestled with the structural forces that affect individuals and communities, and we have identified impediments in our own context. The continued journey is to pursue personal, communal, and systemic change in our spheres of influence.

Pivot 7: We have examined the shift from maintenance to movement. We have embraced the pursuit of our calling over career. We have considered our connection to grassroots movements, leveraging our power and prophetic voice for those who are marginalized. We have accepted the invitation to live out our truth, love, and justice as an expression of who we are and what we believe. The journey ahead is to become movement makers who practice soul force as a lifestyle.

On the day of our book deadline, I (Shawn) was flying from meetings in Houston back to Chicago to meet up with Reesheda to make our final edits. During the flight, an older gentleman stopped breathing. His two adult daughters who were traveling with him began to cry out for help. Immediately, the flight attendants and other passengers sprang into action. One passenger was a doctor who quickly got out of her seat to check on the unresponsive man. The flight attendants grabbed the medical kit that contained an oxygen tank and IV. Passengers and flight attendants took turns doing chest compressions on the man. When one person got tired, another person would jump up from their seat and continue to pump his chest. The pilots rerouted the plane to the nearest airport. Several passengers comforted the daughters, who were in serious distress. Others, like me, were praying and watching this orchestration of human response and gifts in a moment of crisis.

This continued for about thirty minutes until the plane touched down in a nearby airport. As we arrived at the gate, one of the flight attendants announced, "We have a heartbeat." The whole plane erupted in simultaneous cheers and relief. The paramedics, who were waiting at the gate, rushed on to the plane and took the man to the hospital, where, we were later informed, he became conscious and began breathing on his own. One of the man's daughters exuberantly thanked everyone on the plane as she left, recognizing that it was a collective effort.

I texted Reesheda to let her know I would be delayed, and she told me she was praying for the passenger, the volunteers, and all who were affected. She also texted, "You are witnessing soul force right now!"

She was right. In that moment, people chose to respond courageously, in community, for a common cause. People could have chosen to sit in their seats in fear, afraid that their efforts might fail. Did they really want to be responsible if the man didn't make it? But they didn't think about what would happen to them if they failed; they thought about what would happen to the man if they didn't try.

I was reminded in that moment that soul force really can be tapped into in any circumstance by anyone—whether doctors, ordinary citizens, or flight attendants. No one person saved the man; it was a collective and coordinated effort in which each person contributed their unique gift to the community. I cannot think of a better illustration of soul force than a group of people, representing many different backgrounds and gifts, who refuse to give up until every last one has come alive.

Soul force is our courageous and creative self. It is who we were meant to be. It is who we have dreamed of being.

And now is the time to live. To choose truth, love, community, and justice each day. To move toward the dream and actualize our purpose.

Appendix A

INDICATORS
OF GROWTH FOR
EACH PIVOT

You may be wondering, "But how can I know whether I've made a particular pivot or not? Can I measure my progress?" While growth in each of the seven pivots is not completely quantitative, here are some indicators for each pivot that will help you to determine if you are growing in each one. Take note that some indicators are repeated for more than one pivot. This is to illustrate the ways in which the pivots and your growth in them overlap.

PIVOT 1: FROM FEAR TO FREEDOM

- Fear alone is not enough to *automatically* stop you in your tracks. You recognize it and still give yourself the opportunity to consider moving forward.
- You ask yourself the question, "What am I afraid of?" You can allow yourself to unpack what is creating the fear. You are able to sort out what is real and what is not, to address what is real, and then to decide from there if, how, or when to proceed.

- More and more, you can look back on instances in which you were afraid and did not let the fear stop you from moving forward.
- Other people begin to ask you "Weren't you afraid?" about experiences you have now had and the stories you share about those experiences. This is a moment for you to speak into the life of another about how you have grown from fear to freedom.
- You are able to take stock of people, places, opportunities, ideas, and relationships that you now have, some or all of which you did not engage in or consider in times past.

PIVOT 2: FROM BARRIERS TO BRIDGE BUILDING

- You are able to take stock of people, places, opportunities, ideas, and relationships that you now have, some or all of which you did not engage in or consider in times past.
- You orchestrate relationships between people, organizations, and communities that trust you but that were previously unfamiliar with one another.
- Rather than protecting or preserving your gifts and talents from competitors, you now see people and organizations who share your passions as potential collaborators.
- You have shifted from defending your position to asking questions in an effort to better understand other viewpoints and perspectives.
- You no longer have to benefit from every partnership or relationship you help to foster; rather, you become fulfilled in knowing that you have served as a connector, though the connection may not benefit you directly at all.

PIVOT 3: FROM SELF-CENTEREDNESS TO SOLIDARITY

- You no longer have to benefit from every partnership or relationship you help to foster; rather, you become fulfilled in knowing that you have served as a connector, though the connection may not benefit you directly at all.

- You are moving from preservation to redistribution of your gifts, skills, and talents.
- You experience discomfort, challenge, or sacrifice on behalf of others, even if the issue for which you are taking a stand is not one that affects you directly.
- You rally your circle of influence on behalf of others, even if the issue for which you are taking a stand is not one that affects you or them directly.
- You recognize the ways in which you have become uncomfortable and allow yourself to make the sacrifice, knowing that what you are sacrificing for is worth the discomfort you are experiencing.

PIVOT 4: FROM HURT TO HOPE

- You connect and create more often than you complain and critique, recognizing your own agency to bring forth change.
- You inspire others to participate in transformation of self and others, allowing your magnetic energy to attract other agents of hope.
- You invite critical friends to hold you accountable to being vulnerable and authentic with yourself and others.
- You experience increased transparency and vulnerability in your conversations and relationships. You share parts of yourself that you were unwilling to share before.
- There is tangible evidence of creativity and innovation in your life and the lives of those you touch.

PIVOT 5: FROM CONSUMING TO CREATING

- You have become more thoughtful about what you purchase or "buy into" and how your choices affect people, the environment, and the world.
- You often ask yourself, "Is there a more cost-effective, equitable, or collaborative way to get this done?" And then you do the work of both finding and implementing the answer.
- You are moving away from criticizing what already exists toward channeling that energy into discovering what could be.

- You are shifting from simply accepting mediocrity to iterating ideas: building on what is already present to make it more equitable, sustainable, and collaborative.
- You embrace calculated risk in exchange for the possibility of a better quality of life for all.

PIVOT 6: FROM CHARITY TO CHANGE

- You truly believe in the capacity of all humanity to positively influence their own destiny and transformation.
- You relinquish power to others to serve as their own change agents.
- You take on a posture of humility to ask questions, listen, and hear the voices and plans of those who are traditionally marginalized.
- You empower others to take over your role in the future and work to build and develop indigenous, sustainable leadership.
- You create accountability for yourself toward the transformation you are seeking in your own life.

PIVOT 7: FROM MAINTENANCE TO MOVEMENT

- You refuse to employ simple solutions for complex challenges.
- You forego the superficial (temporary fixes, surface-level relationships, legalistic responses, transactional interactions), and create what endures (sustainable solutions, authentic relationships, holistic responses, transformational interactions).
- You use your prophetic voice in ways that galvanize and mobilize equity and justice.
- You embrace the journey over the destination, recognizing that the process holds as much or more benefit than the end goal.
- You recognize that you are in the movement but you don't own it.

Appendix B

INTERNAL AND
EXTERNAL
DIMENSIONS OF
SOUL FORCE

Because soul force emanates from the inside out, leading to both personal and social transformation, it is helpful to see the distinctions between the internal and external dimensions of soul force for each of the seven pivots. We often prioritize one dimension over the other, but soul force encompasses both.

(See table, next page)

B.1 Relationship between internal and external soul force

	Internal soul force	External soul force
Fear to freedom	Overcoming personal fears and developing inner courage to face them: being willing to "do it afraid"	Exposing societal fears that lead to oppression and courageously confronting them in the public square
Barriers to bridge building	Deconstructing personal barriers and opening up to differences	Dismantling physical barriers and setting tables for diverse exchanges
Self-centeredness to solidarity	Examining personal self-interest; developing a social conscience; practicing empathy	Prioritizing the common good in institutions, politics, and economics; practicing common concern for humanity across geographical borders
Hurt to hope	Processing woundedness toward inner healing and hope through discovering resilience	Providing health standards and supportive services for the well-being of communities, people groups, and nations
Consuming to creating	Generating and practicing soulful well-being	Nurturing sustainability of the planet for generations to come
Charity to change	Practicing discipline and accountability: politely insisting on the truth of your power to be transformed	Implementing authentic indigenous leadership development and equitable distribution of power, wealth, and access
Maintenance to movement	Moving steadily and committing to long-term growth; aligning inner realities with love, truth, justice, and collective impact	Committing to long-term change and collective impact

Appendix C

DISCUSSION AND REFLECTION QUESTIONS

These questions can help both individuals and groups consider the chapters more deeply.

AN ENTRY INTO SOUL FORCE
1. What posture is necessary for anyone interested in fully tapping into soul force?
2. How is soul force relevant in your ordinary, everyday life?
3. What does your own soul force have the potential to unlock?

PIVOT 1: FROM FEAR TO FREEDOM
1. In what ways is the pivot from fear to freedom perhaps the most significant pivot to make?
2. When have you ever "done it afraid?" What was the outcome? What can you take from that experience?
3. What does a life of freedom have to offer you that living a life consumed by fear cannot? Explain.

PIVOT 2: FROM BARRIERS TO BRIDGE BUILDING

1. What are some barriers that have been passed on to you by people who meant well and wanted to protect you but that may no longer be required or relevant in your life?
2. What is the difference between barriers and boundaries? How can you employ boundaries in a way that promotes bridge building?
3. What is required in order to live a life committed to bridge building?

PIVOT 3: FROM SELF-CENTEREDNESS TO SOLIDARITY

1. How has self-preservation led to a fulfilling, joyful life experience? Or has it not? Explain.
2. What do you currently sacrifice? How are you currently experiencing discomfort to be in solidarity with people who experience inequity and injustice?
3. What does it look like to embody solidarity? How do you know? Have the people you hope to stand in solidarity with had an opportunity to speak into this vision with you?

PIVOT 4: FROM HURT TO HOPE

1. Whom do you know who is feeling hurt, pain, and hopelessness and is not yet authentically ready to move into hopefulness? What posture do you take? What posture would you want others to take if it were you?
2. What kinds of thoughts, experiences, ideas, or interactions move one from hurt to hope? How might you foster this kind of pivot in yourself? In others?
3. What is the purpose of hope? Is there any value in hope for the sake of it, or is there a deeper meaning or purpose for hope?

PIVOT 5: FROM CONSUMING TO CREATING

1. What are the things—tangible (money, homes, cars) or intangible (power, position, voice at the table)—that you possess but either do not need or do not need as badly as another really does? What makes you hold on to them? What would happen if you gave them away or shared them?

2. What have you metaphorically ingested without even thinking about it? What values, ideas, or beliefs have you just accepted all your life that you have never truly examined? Why haven't you examined them? What would happen if you did?

3. Often, when we think of creating, we think of tangible things. Where in your life are you creating space for people who are not like you? Where are you creating room for relationships across differences? What does it look like for you to do this mutually, reciprocally, authentically? How will you know if you have done it in a way that honors the other?

PIVOT 6: FROM CHARITY TO CHANGE

1. When and under what circumstances is charity helpful or beneficial? When is it not?

2. Think about a concrete time that you've been in a community or setting different from your usual one. What did you notice? What might you have failed to notice?

3. How can you train yourself to see strengths, gifts, and assets in individuals and communities?

4. Brainstorm a list of all the elements that must be present to produce lasting, effective, equitable change.

PIVOT 7: FROM MAINTENANCE TO MOVEMENT

1. What is most troubling about maintaining the status quo in our country and in our world?

2. In the spirit of movement making, whom are you coaching toward transformation? Who is coaching you? If you don't have either of these relationships, why do you think that is? If you do, how will you continue to develop them so that you are constantly growing and being transformed?

3. What is the value of a movement, practically speaking? Why do we need to continue to foster movements, even as we continue to produce organizations and institutions? What movements are you a part of? If none, why not?

ACKNOWLEDGMENTS

We would like to thank Herald Press and, more specifically, Valerie Weaver-Zercher, our editor, for the tireless, unwavering support and expertise on the process and completion of *Soul Force*. We certainly could not have done this without you. We are also appreciative of each and every person who courageously and authentically shared their stories with us for this book. The manifestation of the South African version of *ubuntu* truly rang through: We are because you are!

I (Reesheda) want to thank my community of support and encouragement on this journey. Affiliates of CFA, CCDA, SLCC, Mission Year, Crosspoint, The Parish Collective, Church on the Block, At the Table, OPRFCF Leadership Lab, and of course, L!VE Café have spoken into my life, and they journey with me in ways that are invaluable. Without my community, I would not have a story to tell. This book is possible because I have been blessed to share my life with you! To Shawn: you made it easy to coauthor, and I am grateful for the regenerative soul force we experienced during this project. Finally, thank you, Darrel, Datrianna, Micaiah, and Olivia. This has been a long and sacrificial journey for us all, and I appreciate the sacrifices you made so that I could take on this project.

I (Shawn) want to thank my community of friends, family, Mission Year coworkers, and co-laborers who inspire and support me daily. I am thankful to the many mentors, community leaders, and global activists who have taught me longevity, integrity, and hope-filled resistance and who have gracefully poured into my life directly and indirectly over the last forty years. I want to thank Michelle Patterson, founder of Heart Peace Counseling Center, for sharing resources for this book and for always believing in your little brother. To Reesheda: I am grateful for your trust, friendship, and collaborative spirit. The force of your soul is contagious and changing the world! Last, I want to thank my wife, Jen, for showing me what love, creativity, and generosity looks like every day and for being my equal and partner on this journey of life.

THE AUTHORS

Reesheda Graham-Washington is the executive director of Communities First Association (cfapartners.org), a national faith-based nonprofit committed to asset-based community development, and the founder and CEO of L!VE Café (livexclamation. com), an artisanal destination coffee shop that focuses on community transformation and bridge building. A facilitator of effec-

tive posturing and difficult conversations, Graham-Washington is a minister and educator, and served as an administrator for Chicago Public Schools. A resident of Berwyn, Illinois, she shares her heart for service with her husband and three daughters. Follow her on Twitter and Instagram (@livexclamation).

Shawn Casselberry is a passionate advocate for God's justice, writer, activist, and Executive Director for Mission Year, a leading national Christian ministry that trains Christian young adults to love God, love people, and be a force for justice in the city (missionyear.org). Trained in Kingian nonviolence and community organizing,

Casselberry actively works for peace and reconciliation in the city. He has a passion for mentoring young adults and mobilizing the church around issues of racial and economic justice, particularly issues of mass incarceration and youth violence. With a master's degree in world missions and evangelism from Asbury Theological Seminary and a doctor of ministry degree in building beloved community from McCormick Theological Seminary, he is committed to speaking truth to power and equipping the church to be a prophetic witness in the world. He and his wife, Jen, live in the North Lawndale neighborhood on Chicago's West Side. Follow him on Twitter (@scasselberry) and see what he's up to at ShawnCasselberry.com.